CW00357925

John Burns and Peter [...]
of more than 30 years, [...]
each other. They ther[...]
this case doubly, qual[...]
love, courtship, marr[...]
despair, anguish, ang[...]
parts of the Battle of [...]

Whilst they would vigorously deny that any of the disasters or mis-deeds recounted within these pages reflect their own behaviour or in any way parallel their own experiences, they can categorically state that these sort of things really do happen to ordinary, everyday, loving (and not-so-loving) folk.

Although claiming to fit neatly into the ordinary, everyday, loving-folk category, both the authors admit that, as journalists on the staff of a national daily newspaper, they have over the years been forced to spend a good deal of time away from home. This may explain why their marriages have lasted so long.

John Burns was born in Belfast and worked on a number of local newspapers before becoming the first – and, to date, only – provincial journalist to win the coveted News Reporter of the Year Award, for his coverage of the Ulster troubles. Armed with this title, and a singularly tacky presentation desk set, he moved to London ten years ago in search of fame and fortune. He is still looking. He lives in Finchley, North London, with his wonderful, faithful, hard-working, adorable, tolerant, supportive, intuitive, extraordinarily beautiful, sexy, witty and long-suffering wife Rita and two young sons.

Peter Mason was born in Melbourne, Australia, and has lived in England off and on since 1959. He was named Reporter of the Year in the 1980 British Press Awards for his coverage of the Iranian Embassy siege. Despite an almost total preoccupation with such dangerous and time-consuming activities as hang-gliding, parachuting, windsurfing, sailing and getting locked-up in foreign jails and deported from various African states he is still married to his wonderful, faithful, hard-working, adorable, tolerant, supportive, intuitive, extraordinarily beautiful, sexy, witty and long-suffering English wife Sheila. They live by the sea in Broadstairs, Kent, with their two teenage sons.

John Burns and
Peter Mason

TROUBLE AND
STRIFE

CORGI BOOKS

TROUBLE AND STRIFE
A CORGI BOOK 0 552 12770 1

First publication in Great Britain

PRINTING HISTORY
Corgi edition published 1987

Text material copyright © John Burns and Peter Mason 1986
Illustrations copyright © Edward McLachlan 1986

This book is set in 10/11pt Plantin

Corgi Books are published by Transworld Publishers
Ltd., 61–63 Uxbridge Road, Ealing, London W5 5SA, in
Australia by Transworld Publishers (Aust.) Pty. Ltd.,
15–23 Helles Avenue, Moorebank, NSW 2170, and in New
Zealand by Transworld Publishers (N.Z.) Ltd., Cnr. Moselle
and Waipareira Avenues, Henderson, Auckland.

Printed and bound in Great Britain by
Cox & Wyman Ltd., Reading, Berks.

Contents

ACKNOWLEDGEMENTS

The authors would like to express their sympathy and condolences to courting, engaged and married couples everywhere. Without them this book would not have been possible. They would also like to thank all their just-married, still-married and not-quite-married friends, and their many friends and colleagues in Fleet Street, who came to their aid with their own tales of the sublime and the ridiculous. Special thanks to Maurice Dodd, Richard Jones, Peter Muller, Terry Herbert and Jack Kay for their invaluable assistance with ideas, research and guidance; and to Rita and Sheila who typed the early drafts, corrected our numerous mistakes and word-processed the finished product. Thanks, too, to Tracey and Simon, Flo and Bob, Fred and Hilda, Romeo and Juliet, Tony and Petal, John and Louise and Paul and Sarah, Charles and Di, Flossie and Bill, Timothy and Bernard, Jason and Esmerelda, Helen and Chuck, Bob, Doreen and Camilla, Nigel and Sam, Ronnie and Nancy, Bert and Doris, Anthony and Cleopatra, Harry and Marge, Jeremy and Clarissa, the Marquis de Sade, Liz and Phil, Fiona, Samantha, Lorraine, Elizabeth, Suzie, Jill, Geraldine, Melissa, Jane, Allison and Genevieve. And to all those who asked to remain anonymous. To all of you, this book is dedicated.

Foreword

Ever since Eve took that first, fateful bite of The Apple, Man has been having trouble with his Trouble and Strife. Of course, Woman hasn't exactly had it all that easy, either.

Trouble and Strife is all about that quirky, often bizarre, sometimes uproarious, occasionally blissful and, despite all the odds, invariably fruitful relationship between the Male and Female of the species.

It takes an irreverent, sideways look at that most talked-about of all institutions, marriage, and the often irrational effect it has on its participants, and is crammed full of all those stories that every self-respecting Best Man would just love to tell at the wedding reception, but doesn't know how.

Now, armed with this novice's guide to the pitfalls and pleasures of matrimony, no Best Man (or Best Woman) need ever feel at a loss for words again.

Words about how to avoid falling victim to the sort of errant behaviour that led to three of Maria Velten's four husbands succumbing to her blueberry puddings, made to a secret recipe which included a liberal dose of poison. Asked by the judge why she hadn't simply divorced them, Frau Velten replied: 'That would have caused too many inconveniences.'

Or how to *really* get at your mother-in-law; like sailor Alan Wilkinson, who ran over his while parking the car, then panicked when he realized what had happened and promptly did it again. 'He seemed determined to get me,' joked Mrs Elsie Dalton, nursing two broken legs. 'But you've got to laugh, haven't you?'

Then there was the husband who hired a hit-man to kill his wife, handed over the money, and then found that he'd been conned. He was so enraged that he went to the police to complain – and found himself up on a conspiracy-to-murder charge.

Mind you, marriage, to some people is more a way of life than a life of bliss. Some people simply don't know when to stop. Like Glynn Wolfe, the world's most married man, who remarked, after calling it a day with wife No. 26: 'Marriage is like a bus. You miss one and down the road comes another.'

Culled from the pages of history, the romantic – and the not-so-romantic – novel, and the world's press, and plucked from the ether of everyday life, *Trouble and Strife* traces the rocky progress of the Battle of the Sexes and gives a graphic, occasionally mind-boggling and always amusing account of some of the zanier episodes of contemporary courtship, love, marriage, and all the other bits that go with it. For better or for worse.

Introduction

Let us be frank and earnest about this; History is unfair to women. It's always mankind this, mankind that and mankind the other. Sometimes you'd think we managed it all on our own.

But just stop for a moment and think upon womankind. Consider her ways, her many gifts which, though she would modestly deny it, played so vital a role in getting us into the state we're in today.

For example, who, do you think, invented the wheel . . . some Cro-Magnon handyman? Bunk! It was turned out by a woman.

She crashed it on her test drive.

And it was not until a thousand years later, when a man invented the GT badge, that he pieced the thing together again and got it rolling.

Or how about fire? It, too, was sparked off by a woman, so she could ruin the dinner while her stone-age spouse was out getting stoned with the boys.

And the plough? Again inspired by a woman. She devised it to sow potatoes while her old man was out planting the horses.

And on through the ages we find many more instances of feminine ingenuity: The Headache . . . the oldest, yet still the most popular form of birth control; the Alcoholic Drink . . . a close runner-up to the above; the Twin Bed; and so on.

But all the while, as the pearl-grey dawn of pre-history broke over the world, womankind was building up to her supreme invention . . . *The Marriage.*

Before this, women were civil-tongued, mild-mannered souls, fond of painting themselves up like Boy George and trying on each other's bearskins.

Then all that changed. Suddenly there were in-laws, out-laws, all sorts of riff-raff cluttering up the neighbourhood. Husbands would come home of an evening to find some poncy herbert in a leopardskin jockstrap painting rude things on cave walls.

Wives took to gadding about on scaled-down wheels, to the alarm of all and sundry. They began to witter on about clothes

9

('You know I can't wear these old dodo feathers . . . they're as dead as a sabre-toothed tiger'). That sort of thing.

The more radical invented muesli and pushed off to Greenham Common to protest about the bow and arrow.

Some wives began to find fault in their partners. 'You've abandoned me,' they wailed. 'You don't club me any more.'

Some took matters – and the clubs – into their own hands, and thus was invented the rolling pin. There were other, more gentle sisters who tried to woo their men with love potions, the chief ingredient of which was the ground horn of the mastodon. Which is the chief reason why there aren't all that many mastodons around these days – or Stone-Age men either, for that matter.

And then there were the altogether more ruthless women; the sort who took violent objection to the way their mate pulled hairs out of his ears and cracked fleas on his belly.

To these bitter women fell the awful invention of poison. Many a fine grown man of four foot six or so went to his Maker by way of a mess of coelacanth soup with a garnish of deadly nightshade.

Of course, all this happened a long, long time ago. We were primitives then, savages barely out of the trees. Today Mankind can look itself and civilization in the eye.

As for Womankind, well, read on MacDuff . . .

For Love or Money

Times are tough everywhere. It used to be a man's ambition to find a job, meet a nice girl and settle down.

Now there aren't any jobs to be found, what's a man to do?

Well, he could always marry money, we suppose. But beware, that's not such a soft number as it appears.

Just look at the House of Windsor, one of the richest bunch of in-laws you could ever hope to meet.

Did you know that *every* man who marries into the Royal Family gets a gastric ulcer after only a few weeks?

Few people know that, barring Prince Philip, Lord Snowdon, Mark Phillips etc etc . . .

For Love or Money

. . . can't buy me love

You'd think by now some nice girl would have snapped up Wayne Van Velsor; well, if not a nice girl at least one with a fine sense of the economic realities of this world.

Wayne is a bachelor, a lonesome one, who labours under the popular delusion that money *can* buy you love.

To this end the poor sap has acquired writers' cramp and a sadly depleted bank balance. His peculiar habit is to advertise his singular state on just about every dollar bill he can lay his mitts on.

Wayne types his phone number and the heartfelt plea: 'Single man, 36, wishes to meet a woman 21 to 36, to date and have a lasting relationship.'

In just five years he has put into circulation 13,853 such dollar bills. That adds up to not a kick in the pants off £10,000.

Says he proudly: 'I have 141 note books full of serial numbers.'

And a fat lot of good they've done him. At the last count, 3,600 women have rung his Little Falls, New Jersey, number, presumably to ask if he's got much more of where this came from.

Wayne has weeded them down to only 23 he bothered to date, and none of them was worth the money.

He sighs: 'I'm still hopeful of meeting Miss Right. It is interesting talking to all these girls, but I guess I'm just picky.'

In which case he might be better off plugging his needs on 100-dollar bills.

If you are a woman who is married or living with a man you can claim invalid care allowance now. – **Citizens Advice Bureau poster.**

The Dear Hunter

The passionate gamekeeper wanted only to play things by the book; in his case the volume concerned being *Lady Chatterley's Lover*.

As any devotee of that spirited yarn is well aware, your gamekeeper's true position in life is largely horizontal.

Sadly for all concerned, especially herself, the aristocratic mistress of Marceau Couter was no student of English Lit.

Their liaison kicked off in the approved style, with Jacqueline Bourgeois meeting him on a hunting trip in the Loire valley.

She was a chic, rich woman of the world, a divorcee in her late thirties, with a mansion in Paris and a château somewhere in the family.

Marceau was hardly Monsieur Cool; the burly son of simple peasant stock, he had quit school at 13 and gone off to work in the forest.

He was also 14 years older than Jacqueline and already had a wife. But love, or lust at least, conquered all. Marceau quit home to set up house with his mistress.

The abandoned Francine Couter had some famous last words to say on the subject, warning her errant mate: 'If you go with her you'll live to regret it.'

Marceau said phooey and off he went.

For a while the lovers got on like a house on fire. But then the rough edges, which first attracted Jacqueline to him, began to cause friction. Like a million foolish women before her, she tried to change her man.

Instead of just rural romps with her pet gamekeeper, Jacqueline insisted he shared her other life in Paris. She took to dragging the protesting Marceau around Parisian parties, showing her rough diamond to all the girls.

He held her race card at the Bois de Boulogne, her art catalogues at the galleries, her hand at the opera. He even held his temper at the soirees where they examined him like a prize bull.

Then Jacqueline overdid things – she made the poor fool carry her bags as she shopped in the boutiques of the Faubourg St. Honoré.

Sure enough, Marceau cracked. Back in their sylvan lovenest he told her: 'No more. Let me look after the estate while you go alone.'

Jacqueline, who was a bit squiffy at the time, put down her glass and pulled a hunting rifle on him. Or so he later told the gendarmes.

He panicked, snatched another gun and drilled her clean through the heart.

His next move was even more daft. Marceau ran hotfoot back to his wife. And was she the forgiving sort? Was she hell. She phoned the law pretty damn toute suite and handed him over.

Marceau is presently examining the folly of his ways while he sits out a 13-year jail sentence for murder.

And if Francine ever comes to visit him, you can bet your boots it's just to say: 'I told you so . . .'

Dear George, I have waited three years for you but now I have met a GI. We are going away together for a while – but don't worry too much because he says when you come home he will buy you the motorbike you always wanted. Jill. – **Letter to a British soldier in German POW camp**.

Six appeal

It was money well spent, said Mrs Ellen Pike with a certain grim satisfaction. It bought her the following ad in her local newspaper at Worksop, Notts:

'Ellen Pike, nee Waddell, is pleased to announce her divorce from Geoffrey. She wishes to thank all her family for their tremendous support.'

Later 27-year-old Ellen added: 'I am delighted to be rid of him at last. That's why I spent the best £6 of my life on the ad.'

Over to ex-husband Geoff, who said of their differences: 'It was six of one and half-a-dozen of the other.'

Graham and Caroline Keith wish to thank everyone who helped at their wedding and for all the lovely gifts received. Thanks also to Victor who helped to make it two very enjoyable nights. – **From the Personal Column, *Shetland Times***.

Exchange and marked

Disenchanted wife Beverley Pink couldn't exactly be accused of calling her husband worthless. The way she saw it, he was worth all of £25. Top whack.

And having settled on a price, Beverley, 25, stuck an advert in the 'Nothing over £30' column of her local paper at Southsea, Hants.

She offered: 'Eccentric husband with odd personality, unusual looking although fathers beautiful kids. £25 or offers.

Would consider swopping.'

Her aggrieved partner, Peter, 41, railed: 'I think she's being silly. She was a moody wife. I tried to concentrate on the marriage but my business got into trouble.'

The union foundered after only six weeks. But Beverley conceded: 'He did give me a beautiful boy. I suppose he had to do something properly.'

Her advert attracted only one reply, and that from a woman offering a South American sloth in part exchange. Rather fitting, thought Beverley: 'He was an idle husband,' said she.

Gone fishing

Garth Weldall's missus got pretty fed up with her old man's pursuits, too. So when she hit on the idea of putting all his

17

huntin', shootin' and fishin' gear up for sale, she decided to solve the problem of his continual absences from home once and for all – and threw him in with the deal as well.

What she didn't bargain for, however, was the overwhelming response to the advert she placed in her hometown newspaper in Isanti, Minneapolis, under the heading: Sporting goods.

'Help wanted,' the ad ran. 'Husband for sale, cheap. Comes complete with hunting and fishing equipment. Also one pair of jeans, two shirts, a lab retriever and 25 pounds of deer meat. Not home much between September and January and April through October. Will consider trade.'

Shortly afterwards, according to Garth, a 27-year-old mechanic, 'people went nuts.'

The phone rang non-stop for days, with women calling up in droves to see if they could do a deal over action-man Garth, or at least arrange a trade-in.

By the time the story got picked up by the local radio station Mrs Weldall knew it was time to set things right. So the following week, under the same heading, she placed the following: 'No help wanted. Due to overwhelming response, not for sale or trade, one dearly loved husband whose birthday joke got out of hand. Sorry, Hon.'

Mind you, the enterprising Mrs Weldall could have done quite well out of the deal. Many of the callers were men who wanted to know if they could drop in on her in case she succeeded in peddling her husband.

Putting the boot in

Just in case you should ever need to know the going rate for a bride in Soviet Central Asia, the Tadjikistan Communist newspaper reports that a couple there flogged off their daughter for 2,000 roubles (£2,000), 40 pairs of galoshes, a cow, two sheep, 12 kerchiefs, 60 metres of cloth and two sacks of rice.

One can only hope they chucked rice, not galoshes over the new Mr and Mrs.

18

Deadlier than the Male

. . . Such was Mr Kipling's exceedingly good advice about the female of the species; others have noted that Hell hath no fury like a woman scorned.

But we rather like Frank Sinatra's barbed shaft when an ex-girlfriend wrote a book about their steamy love life.

Ol' Blue Eyes growled: 'Hell hath no fury like a hustler with a literary agent.'

Deadlier than the Male

Mane chance

The booze was dirt cheap, the nights were balmy, and, what the hell, he was on holiday after all. Fuelled with such impeccable logic and a pocketful of pesetas, Robert Dimart sallied forth for yet another night on the town.

Behind him, in their holiday bungalow on the Costa Blanca, seethed Madame Dimart, fed up to the back teeth with her mate's fondness for the vino.

She brooded on the inevitable. Sure enough, several hours later when the cafes shut up shop, Robert came reeling home again with a song in his heart and strong drink on his breath.

Madame D. took one look at her ossified spouse and let him have it. Cruel words were said, most of which were lost on Robert as he was in no fair state to listen.

With one last barbed shaft, she stormed off to sleep in the spare room, slamming the door behind her. Robert kicked off his shoes, shrugged out of his clothes and pitched into his lonely bed.

Sometime in the middle of the night his drunken slumber was disturbed. Through mists of alcohol he tried to figure out what had wakened him.

It was his wife. And she was licking his ear.

It wasn't one of those little half-hearted little nibbles of the lobe either. This was a full-blooded licking and her hot breath spoke of passion.

Sacre bleu, thought Robert, for he was a Frenchman. She has forgiven me already.

And gallant Gaul that he was, he turned to embrace her, only to find himself sharing a bed with a lady even fiercer than Madame Dimart when roused – a full-grown lioness.

With a shriek Robert was out of bed in one bound and off down the road like a fairly briskish bullet.

But the Parisian businessman had not legged it very far before he fetched up against a pair of local policemen. They were observant fellows. First, they noticed that Robert was wearing only his little pink skin, finely beaded with perspiration.

21

They commented too upon the alcoholic aura which seemed to surround him. Finally, when panting Robert began to tell them there was a lion in his bed, they exchanged significant looks.

'We've got a right one here,' seemed to be the gist of their thoughts. 'Let's find him a nice little cell and a litre of black coffee.'

But even as the bracelets were being produced, the lioness herself strolled unconcernedly out of Robert's front door.

She was in a matey mood and, after reinforcements were called pronto, was soon recaptured. All the while Madame Dimart slept on.

Police later found the amorous lioness had escaped from her trainer's car. He was subsequently prosecuted for the neglect of his passenger's safety.

Robert's wife took more taming than the beast, at first refusing point blank to believe the incident had ever happened. One imagines she made cheap cracks about pink elephants and little green men and so forth.

When finally convinced she was still miffed – she didn't think it at all complimentary that Robert had mistaken a lioness for her.

The marriage suffered a setback in 1965 when the husband was killed by the wife. – **Extract from the *New Law Journal*.**

The proof of the pudding . . .

Every once in a while a Krefeld, West German, housewife liked to get out the rolling pin and dish out something special for her loved ones.

Maria Velten prided herself on blueberry puddings made to her own secret recipe.

She never tasted the things herself, which accounts for why Maria is still with us but her father, her aunt, and her second, third and fourth husbands are not.

The murders, spread over 20 years, went undetected until she enrolled hubby No. 4 in her poison pudding club. When arrested, Maria confessed to the other murders.

Asked by her trial judge why she did not simply divorce them, the redoubtable Frau Velten replied, 'That would have brought too many inconveniences.'

Her first husband managed to avoid Maria's blueberry pudding. He got himself killed in the war.

Rational thinker

Judge for yourself, but the way we figure it, Mrs Jessie Pennington was being the very soul of reasonableness when she described her ex-husband's divorce petition as ludicrous.

Earlier the appalling Bernard Pennington had set about his wife of three months with a machete, leaving her for dead.

With a savagery which hardly bears thinking about, he slit her throat, cut off two of her fingers and left her permanently scarred.

Yet from his prison cell where he is currently serving life, *he* successfully sued for divorce – on the grounds of *her* unreasonable behaviour.

Mrs Pennington, 31, of Doncaster, Yorks 'died' twice on the operating table and needed 800 stitches. Her facial muscles remain partially paralysed.

She argues: 'Surely I should have been able to get an automatic divorce from him after what he did to me.'

But when Pennington filed his suit, she was too scared to fight it because she would have had to face him in court.

'I've been spared that ordeal,' said Mrs Pennington.

Sleep of the unjust

Some guilty husbands blab out the name of their illicit sweethearts as they sleep. Guiseppe Larroni went one worse. He started rabbitting on about his best friend.

Considering the aforesaid best friend, Tomasso Gemma, was dead these past six years, Guiseppe's wife, Teresa, was deeply interested in his unconscious babble.

And when it is recalled that Teresa was once married to the late Tomasso, you can imagine she was agog indeed.

As her sleeping spouse rambled away in bed beside her, she recalled that night six years earlier when her first husband died.

Guiseppe had rushed into the Police Station in the southern Italian port of Brindisi, shouting: 'There has been a murder. Someone has shot my friend Tomasso.'

And so there was, and so somebody did. But who and why the police never did find out.

In the meantime the stricken Guiseppe started making sympathy calls on his dear friend's young widow.

He was kind, he was considerate, and, after a decent interval, he was courting Teresa. In due course they wed and the marriage was considered a sound one.

Until the night Guiseppe cried out in his sleep.

'I want Teresa,' he blurted. 'And that's why you're dead.'

'Curious,' thought she, and forgot all about it. Until the next night. And the night after that. At last it dawned on her that he was reliving the night of the murder.

Now it was her turn to call in the Brindisi police and, after a minor spot of interrogation, Guiseppe confessed all.

He said: 'I loved Teresa so much I had to have her. I knew that if Tomasso was dead I would have a chance.'

After the funeral of a friend, the bereaved husband came up to me at the graveside and thanked me for being there. Without thinking, I replied: 'It's been a pleasure.' At that particular time I could willingly have bitten my tongue off. – **Mrs Phyllis McStay, of Stoke-on-Trent, Staffs, in a letter to the *Daily Express*.**

A fare cop

Greek cabbie Pericles Lambrino was not the happiest of men as he trundled homewards after what should have been a prosperous night.

For Pericles had not a drachma to call his own, having blown his earnings in a card school.

Ahead of him lay the daunting prospect of explaining all this to his wife, a redoubtable lady, much given to boxing his ears and calling him offensive names. Indeed, so fierce was her tongue and so fiery her temper that Pericles had taken to working all the hours God sent just to keep out of her way. Now what was he to do.

'Eureka!' exclaimed Pericles, 'I'll tell the police I have been robbed. They'll believe me.'

They did too until his missus stormed into the police station and started belabouring him with the sharp end of her umbrella.

'You can't fool me with this robbery nonsense,' cried she. Thump thump.

Nor did he try. He immediately owned up that he had been telling porky pies. In the circumstances the police thought he had had enough punishment and didn't bother to charge him with wasting their time.

But if it ever happens again, Pericles will know what to do: demand police protection, that's what.

Bride and gloom

She was tearful and verging on hysteria when she phoned the police. 'I've lost my husband,' she wailed.

Bearing in mind that she had married the guy only a few hours earlier, this might have sounded like downright carelessness.

But, as the bride explained, they had just checked into their honeymoon hotel in Seattle when he breezed off to fetch a six-pack of beer and some cigarettes. He never came back.

The Washington police had some good news and some bad news. The missing spouse had turned up and he was alive.

But he was under arrest for the knifepoint robbery of a garage attendant. And he had a bullet wound to the leg, occasioned when an officer shot him as he fled.

The police informed his bride they also had his getaway vehicle – the couple's wedding car, still covered with 'Just Married' stickers.

Of all the differences between people, sex must be the greatest divide and the cause of most misconception. – **Shopping Centre Report**.

Poison pen-pal

Around the little township of Tomahawk, Alberta, the lonely prairie stretches away into the blue horizon.

After his beloved wife died, the solitude of it all began to weigh heavily on 50-year-old Henry Joneson.

He yearned for the company of another helpmate on his 900-acre spread. But, as Henry himself observed: 'When would a hard-working farmer find the time to go a-wooing?'

So he placed an ad for a pen-pal in the columns of the Prairie Gazette. There was just one reply, from a lonely widow 2,000 miles away in Nashville, Tennessee.

Ada Wittenmeyer sent Henry her photograph. She was only 39, a fine looking woman. She wrote nice letters that stirred forgotten emotions.

A year and 40 letters later, Henry realized he was in love with his pen-pal. But he was a cautious man and felt he had to see her face to face before he could ask her to become the second Mrs Joneson.

He called directory inquiries for her phone number so he could arrange a date. But the operator was baffled.

She did not have a listing for any Mrs Ada Wittenmeyer of 45 Ezell Pike Street, Nashville. There were no private houses on that street.

Indeed, the only place listed was the De Berry Institute.

So Henry wrote to Ada. She explained that she had been unwell and had been recuperating at the Institute but had not wanted to bother him with her problems.

27

That was good enough for Henry. He wrote back by return of post, sending Ada a $1,000 cheque and his tenderly-worded proposal of marriage.

The next communication from Nashville was a phone call. And it wasn't from Ada.

On the other end was District Attorney Jack Laroque, who told Henry: 'I'm afraid I've some bad news for you.'

The de Berry Institute, he explained, is Nashville's main prison, and Ada is among its most famous inmates.

She was serving life there for the murder of one of her four husbands, 25 years for bumping off another, and was awaiting sentence for killing a third.

Nor was she a reformed character. She told a cellmate she wanted to go on poisoning men for their money and she enjoyed seeing them in agony.

Up in Tomahawk, Alberta, Henry sadly replaced the phone, burned all her letters and returned to the lonesome prairie.

Romancing the Stoned

Love and liquor, like drink and driving, is a pretty dangerous mixture. We are reminded of one Fleet Street photographer who, while covering the Ulster troubles, got monumentally blitzed one night.

So much so that he *seduced* a woman whose resemblance to Quasimodo was more than passing. On the morrow he awoke with the most vindictive of hangovers, only to find the hideous old trout gazing at him in horror.

'My God, what have I done!' *she* exclaimed.

And now for some more sobering thoughts . . .

Romancing the Stoned

The last chord

The Condor Club was always packed to the gills when the striptease artiste Miss Carol Doda made her spectacular entrance – stretched out across a grand piano that slowly descended from the ceiling.

Sadly, the joint was empty when club manager Jimmy 'The Beard' Ferrozzo made his last exit, also stretched out on the old joanna. And what a way to go.

It was after hours and the last highball had been sunk at the topless bar when James felt like sampling the merchandise himself. The goods in question were neatly packaged in the shape of blonde 23-year-old topless dancer Teresa Hill.

They drank a glass or ten, fooled around a bit and it all ended up with 40-year-old Jimmy suggesting they could make sweet music together; or something like that.

Teresa slipped out of her working clothes, which didn't take long, and hopped on board the famous grand, with The Beard doing much the same.

They were having a fairly rumbustious time up there on the piano lid when one of them somehow managed to hit the rise mechanism.

Up and up rose the white baby grand bearing the couple in perfect harmony towards the ceiling.

But by then they were both too drunk or whatever to notice. The Beard's bum hit the ceiling first and Miss Hill hit the roof as soon as she realized what was happening. Not that there was anyone around to hear her.

A sad sight greeted those who eventually came upon the scene. There, pinned to the ceiling was the late Jimmy Ferrozzo, looking considerably thinner than his usual 16 stones. And there, trapped beneath him, was the alive but hysterical Miss Hill, who had had enough of pianos for life.

A San Francisco police inspector explained why she had not jumped off in time: 'She was so intoxicated she doesn't even remember getting on.'

Only The Beard's enormous bulk had come between Teresa and a sticky end, he added.

But next night the show went on as normal. And now if you go to San Francisco you can watch Jimmy Ferrozzo's last trysting place go up and down nightly. But you won't hear anybody playing whoopee on it anymore.

Phoenix Brewery Ltd would like to wish Alan and Linda every success following their recent alterations. – **Ad in the South-ampton Evening Echo**.

Beach bum

Lying on his bum on the beach and watching the topless world go by was beginning to lose its simple pleasure for holiday-maker John Lund.

Frankly, he was browned off with all this sun, sand and skin stuff. What his soul cried out for was a long cool crate of something to sip in the shade.

Understandably, John said nothing of this to his wife. Instead he murmured some nonsense about going for a swim and off he sneaked.

Ingrid Lund basked on, the merry mayhem of summertime Majorca playing in her ears. Time floated by on the wings of seagulls.

All the while John was slaking his thirst in a nearby bar and coming to feel that Majorca was quite a tolerable joint despite the bouquet of burnt flesh.

His mood, when he left the bar, was slightly dampened when he encountered a crowd of sunbathers seeking a lost swimmer.

John opted to give them a hand, but as darkness stole across the beach, everyone agreed the missing man must have perished.

Then Ingrid found the fellow that all the fuss was about. Yes, 'twas John himself. The searchers gazed upon him with disdain and stalked off to eat their paella.

Was Ingrid red-faced? Was she joyous at the return of the prodigal? Well, yes and no. But she got it all out of her system by hauling him off and socking him a beauty in the eye – and serve him jolly well right, too.

32

Ex-London publican seeks lady with pub. Send photo of pub. – **From the personal column of *The Morning Advertiser*.**

Something blue

The wedding reception was in full flood when John Smith sauntered into the Cherry Tree pub, snatched a passing glass of champagne and a cigarette and set about enjoying himself.

Some several glasses later, it dawned on everyone that Smith was not among the invited. Indeed, when challenged on that point he pulled a knife.

It was not the wisest of moves. Almost all the 100 guests were police officers, not least the bride and groom.

Smith's knife act earned him three months. The couple, one hopes, are happily serving life.

Love and porridge

Had bachelor Bob Norton been a soap powder, he would have come boxed in the large economy size; had he been champagne, he would have been a magnum. At least.

As it was, he was just a human being, which meant he was plain fat. And he wasn't all that proud of it.

Even worse, his girlfriend, Dawn, made it patently clear she had no intention of getting herself married to a 14½-stone blob. But if he shed a stone or three . . .

So Bob gave it a try. And failed. He explained: 'The trouble is, when I get the taste I cannot stop. I will drink 15 pints in a session and then go home and eat my way through the larder.'

He had to confess, his willpower was no match for his appetite. But if he could go somewhere where there was no beer, where there were no second helpings, no jumbo burgers with extra chips . . . only where?

The idea struck him like the famous apple which brained Isaac Newton. PRISON!

All he had to do was to get himself jailed, and that was a piece of cake. Bob rolled down to his local bank, smashed a few windows and rang the police.

When the officers arrived he told them: 'I have just bust two windows. Put the handcuffs on. I want to be sent away for three months so that I can lose some weight.'

Obliging magistrates remanded him in custody for three weeks but Bob's first taste of porridge was not all to his liking.

When he reappeared before a West Bromwich court on the adjourned case, Bob was still his old podgy self, still all of 14½ stones.

He sorrowfully reported: 'They feed you lots of puddings and rice and potatoes. There is no chance to lose weight there.'

Ah for the days of bread and water.

Ninty and Olive Bert from Quarry Cottages, would like to thank all family, friends and neighbours for a truly wonderful party for their Golden Wedding anniversary; and, of course, to the council men for erecting the scaffolding to prevent the chimney falling down after the party on Sunday morning. – **Ad in the Ashford, Kent Extra.**

Dough nut

Maybe she should have stuck to the cookbook instead. As it was, a young Hampshire housewife came up with a recipe for disaster when she added cannabis to her cake mixture.

After scoffing them, her schoolteacher husband, Peter Sexton, freaked out and smashed up their home, besides inflicting sundry damage on three cars.

The escapade cost him £250 in fines for one thing and another. Into the bargain his marriage went all to pot too.

Collar and stud . . .

She was a working girl, plying the old profession in the streets of Glasgow, and there's nothing to suggest she didn't come up to expectations.

Unfortunately, tired businessman Alan Henry was a bit of a let down. His performance certainly wasn't going to win any medals.

That is until she gave him a helping handful of black bombers – amphetamines to you or me.

And suddenly he was superstud personified, a sexual athlete who had just scooped the gold and he wanted the world to know. Well, if not the world at least the other guests at the Holiday Inn.

His lustful whoops echoed down the corridors and penetrated the walls. Soon a curious crowd gathered outside his bedroom door as Henry yelled out a bang up-to-the minute report of the current situation twixt he and the lady of the night.

Even after she had pocketed her fee and fled blushing into the night, 21-year-old Henry kept howling for more.

Wearing naught but his jockey briefs, the crazed Henry raced through the corridors, hammering at the doors and roaring for his lost love.

Sooner or later the police arrived. It took four of Strathclyde's finest to corner the runaway ram and slip the bracelets on. And he still kept on bellowing.

On Henry's subsequent appearance before the Sheriff Court where he was fined £650 for possessing the pills and kicking up a rumpus, his solicitor testified to the bombers' efficacy.

Said Mr William Totten: 'They transformed him from wearied impotency to staggering virility.'

Bachelor Henry reckoned that even with the fine, it was money well spent. He said later: 'I'll do it again if I get the chance. Businessmen always let themselves go when they're away from home.'

And in a tribute to his partner of the evening he added: 'The old brass gave me the bombers because I was feeling a bit tired. They gave me a real rush.

'I was going at 100mph and just kept rabbitting. The girl told me the tablets would give me a lift and they certainly did. The running commentary was a bit out of character.'

Quite.

In-Laws, Outlaws

Let's set the record straight about mothers-in-law. They're not such bad old birds at all. Even Les Dawson, who has made it his life's work to slander their name, admits his mum-in-law is the salt of the earth, a woman who can take a joke, which is maybe just as well for him.

You rarely hear about what the poor bride has to put up with in that direction.

Take Rambo's mumbo, otherwise Mrs Jacqueline Stallone. When her little Sylvester fell for the statuesque Brigitte Nielsen, Mrs S. predicted a rocky marriage for them.

Brigitte, she said, was variously a pig, a money grubber and a gold digger. She stormed: 'I didn't raise my son to go off and marry someone like her.'

But off he went and guess who wasn't invited to the wedding reception?

In-laws, Outlaws

Family affair

It was only natural that Bruno Palmisano should feel a shade nervous when he met Angelo, his Sicilian father-in-law.

For starters, Bruno was arm-in-arm with his latest love, the beautiful Franca.

And old Angelo was in the company of his five sons – Flavio, Mario, Pietro, Marcos and Lorenzo.

Into the bargain, Angelo was waving a pistol in a distinctly unfriendly manner.

The moment reminded Bruno unhappily of another occasion when the old man made him an offer he couldn't refuse.

On that occasion the young Romeo felt obliged to marry Angelo's daughter, Anna Maria, whom he had made pregnant.

But only a month after the wedding, Bruno cleared out. And now, four months later, here he was in Turin, 1,000 miles from his lawful wedded, and with another woman.

Angelo stood by an opened car door and ordered: 'Get in.'

Bruno took a look at the gun aimed at his head and in he duly got.

The long journey home to Portigliaro was made in a strained silence. Once back, Bruno was united with Maria and the daughter she had just borne him.

Also much in evidence were his own father and three brothers who advised him in fairly robust terms that he was lucky to be alive, what with bringing dishonour to the family name and all that.

Only the forgiving intervention of Anna Maria had spared him from the trigger-happy Angelo, they said. Suitably chastened, Bruno sat down and signed a statement, swearing he would never again stray.

His resolve lasted all of five days before he hightailed it back to Turin with two car-loads of vengeful relatives in hot pursuit.

A few days after that the Sicilian mob ran Bruno and Franca to earth in their secret love-nest.

This time the in-laws didn't beat about the bush. They told him: 'Come home or die where you stand.'

As the convoy headed south again with Bruno safely aboard, Franca rang the police. And halfway back to Sicily the two cars were halted.

Sorry, officer, there must be some mistake, Bruno told the police.

'I haven't been kidnapped. My relatives are giving me a lift home to my wife and child.'

But the police insisted on investigating further and soon realized they were dealing with a matter of honour.

Even so, they charged the nine members of the posse – and Bruno – with causing a public nuisance and wasting police time.

The latest news from the home front is that Bruno has settled for the quiet life with Anna Maria.

Maybe it's just as well, for Anna Maria has warned him: 'I still love you, but run away again and I will let them kill you.'

Poisoned relations

The embittered husband had just the antidote for his meddling mother-in-law.

She, the 55-year-old West German father-of-three claimed, had poisoned his relationship with his wife. So what better way to make her pay for the break-up of his marriage than to give her a dose of her own medicine: in this case, snake venom.

Armed with a letter from a local herpetarium, and a lethal supply of venom from a Green Mamba – the world's deadliest snake – he set out to wreak his revenge.

As the 78-year-old woman left her Ashaffenburg home for church her son-in-law struck. 'You caused my marriage to break up,' he hissed, as he jabbed her in the shoulder with a needle impregnated with the deadly poison.

The woman died within hours and the man was charged with her murder.

Good Lord!

Of course, not every man dislikes his mother-in-law that much. Certainly not the Marquis of Hertford, whose concern over the disappearance of a portrait of the Marchioness' mother, the 88-year-old Princess Alphonse de Chimay, would appear to give the lie to the hoary old mother-in-law chestnut.

The Graham Rust drawing, which used to enjoy pride-of-place in the Marquis' book-panelled study, went missing after one of the exquisite dinner parties the amiable Marquis is famed for hosting at his stately pile, Ragley Hall.

So incensed was he by the portrait's disappearance that he felt obliged to call in the local Bill, who then had the embarrassing task of interviewing staff and checking out the previous evening's guest list.

'I am extremely fond of my mother-in-law and I would like the picture back,' explained Old Etonian Hertford, a one-time public relations man, after the theft was discovered.

As it transpired, the mystery of the missing portrait proved even funnier than the best of all the old mother-in-law jokes. For the culprit turned out to be none other than . . . Princess Alphonse de Chimay herself!

The Princess, who lives in a house on the 6,000-acre estate, had apparently sneaked into the house and removed the sketch because, she declared afterwards, 'It was little more than a caricature.'

And she revealed that she disliked it so much she had planned to burn it.

'I knew she didn't like the painting, but I didn't know she hated it that much,' explained the Marquis after the work of art was handed back to him in return for a promise that he would never show it in public again.

'Personally, I have always admired it. It never occurred to me that she might take it upon herself to get rid of it.'

And, he added with a pained expression: 'D'you know, she intended to burn it like Lady Churchill did with the Sutherland painting of her husband.'

Insisting that the incident had not affected his feelings towards his mother-in-law, the 54-year-old Marquis declared with typical phlegm: 'The Princess is a wonderful old lady and

I am sure the old chestnut about men not liking their mothers-in-law is just a silly old music hall joke.'

BETTS – On May 26, 1985. Debbie and Keith are delighted to announce the arrival of all of 8½lbs of Benjamin, a brother for Mark. Thanks to all concerned. Keith would also like to announce the imminent arrival of mother-in-law, weighing in at rather more and intending to stay just as long. – **From the Births column of the *Guernsey Evening Press*.**

Indian takeaway

What brides in India need is not so much a rich husband, but a daddy with a bob or two.

Last year some 600 poor girls were bumped off by their in-laws for failing to cough up a big enough marriage settlement. All this despite a Government ban on the ancient custom of dowries.

Incidentally, ancient customs ain't what they used to be. Long gone are the days when all a family demanded of a girl was a goat or two, a chunk of gold and half a pound of darjeeling.

Nowadays pa-in-law is liable to reach for his dagger if she fails to chip in with the likes of a colour TV, a washing machine or a Japanese motorbike.

Another Fein mess

Like many a mother-in-law before her, Vivien Fein regarded her daughter's choice of husband as singularly unsuitable.

All through the couple's short-lived marriage, the redoubtable Mrs Fein could not resist comparing him unfavourably with the less attractive reptiles of this world.

Even after the couple split, Mrs F. nagged on and on. She even filed harassment charges against the unfortunate Jay Marks when he took his children for a day's outing.

Jay was acquitted but promptly sued the old battleaxe for all those years of meddling.

45

'I've had it up to here with her,' he told a Long Island, New York jury.

They agreed and ordered Mrs Fein to pay Jay £5,000 damages. Afterwards the 41-year-old insurance consultant said: 'I'm elated. Up to now a divorced father's only right was to pay and pay.'

Deposit account

She was young enough to be his daughter, but that didn't stop Arnold falling in love with Carol. She was pretty smitten, too.

Now Arnold was an eminently respectable businessman who liked to do things by the book. So when the couple agreed they were made for each other, he did the proper thing: he went to see her dad to ask for Carol's hand in marriage.

Dad took a good look at his prospective son-in-law and said: 'Sure thing.' Or words largely to that effect.

The engagement was duly announced and Carol began window-shopping around Los Angeles with stars in her eyes and a wedding list in her hand.

And then dad, who had rather taken to Arnold, thought it only fair he let the man in on a closely-guarded family secret. Carol, he said, is not my daughter.

You see, he explained, years before doctors had told him he was sterile. But he and his young wife still craved a family of their own.

So they stepped along to the nearest sperm bank, the wife was artificially inseminated, and, after the prescribed period, Carol was born.

The dad spared Arnold nothing in retelling the story. He even named the sperm bank they had consulted.

At which point a sudden terrible thought crossed Arnold's mind. For he recalled that in his impecunious student days he had been a frequent visitor to the same establishment – only as a donor.

After the man-to-man chat, Arnold dashed off and was granted a court injunction which allowed him to browse through the bank's files.

There he found, to his astonishment, he had fathered 807 children.

And one of them was Carol.

The intended wedding between father and daughter was called off and Arnold resolved to do his courting in future far away from Los Angeles and his other 806 children.

Slick humour

Who gives a fig, who utters aught when a groom ends up magnificently oiled on his stag night revels.

But it's altogether a different matter if the bride gets thoroughly oiled half-way through the actual wedding.

And that's the way things threatened to turn out until Berry Wharton asked Birkenhead magistrates to ban one unwelcome guest – his mum.

As Berry explained, he and mother, Mrs Audrey Griffiths, had been more or less at loggerheads since his first marriage foundered some seven years earlier.

Now fianée Christine Roberts had become innocently embroiled in the family squabble and her prospective mother-in-law was threatening to drench the poor girl with engine oil during the ceremony.

Mrs G. was duly barred from the registry office and the bride emerged as pretty as a picture, though hardly a master-piece in oils.

Hits & Mrs

Male chauvinist road hogs will try to persuade you that women drivers are nothing but a bunch of tender gender fender benders.

Women, they say, cannot think ahead, they just don't anticipate enough.

This is so much hogwash of course. Women anticipate like mad. One has only to think of the wife of round-the-world yachtsman Chay Blyth.

Once when he was about to biff off on another of his lonely sea and sky voyages Mrs Blyth prepared for him a parcel 'to be used in an emergency'.

Some months later his yacht, British Steel, was almost pounded to bits in a humdinger of a storm off Cape Horn.

That was emergency enough, thought Chay. He tore open his package in a fever of hope.

'Imagine my feelings,' Chay recalled, 'when I discovered it contained a copy of *The Cruel Sea*.'

Hits & Mrs

Gone with a bang

It was a somewhat bruising encounter when estranged husband and wife Terence and Soraida Kepple bumped into each other again.

Actually, she bumped into him. In her car. And he, poor chap, had his head under the bonnet of his own car when the reunion occurred.

Both were taken to the same Milton Keynes, Bucks, hospital with minor injuries.

Mrs Kepple, still suffering from acute blushing, admitted: 'It was rather embarrassing. I didn't realize it was him because his head was under the bonnet. My car's a write-off.'

Whether the marriage was repaired is not recorded.

A bridge too far

An Idaho couple emerged unscathed from a freak accident in 1968 involving a railway bridge, an out-of-control car and a fast-moving train.

Their car plunged over the parapet, crashed on to the roof of the train which was thundering by below them, and was promptly hurled back onto the bridge from whence it came by the force of the train's momentum.

It wasn't all joy for the unfortunate driver, however. He had to have hospital treatment for a broken nose after his girl-friend, angered by his careless driving, hit him with her handbag.

Man of 38 wishes to meet woman of 30 owning tractor. Please enclose photograph of tractor. – **From the 'Wanted' column of the *Mountain Echo*, South Africa**.

Roll on

Stepping from the mangled remains of his rocket car *Blonde Bombshell* after skidding for more than a quarter-of-a-mile upside down and backwards at 280 miles-an-hour, would-be record breaker Barry Bowles declared ruefully: 'My wife will kill me for this.'

The incident that caused Barry so much angst came during his 1978 attempt to set a new British landspeed record.

After setting off on its first run across Pendine Sands in South Wales the 21-foot long car started to weave from left to right as it accelerated past the 250mph mark.

'The thought flashed through my brains, "You're going to fly boy." The next thing I remember the sky was at my feet and it was really happening,' explained Barry afterwards.

Shedding body panels, fitments and chunks of fibreglass along the way, the car cartwheeled over the sand, took to the air, and then skidded for more than a quarter of a mile on its back. It was still in that position when it hurtled past the one-kilometre marker board at around 280 miles-an-hour.

As it came to rest in a tangled heap of bent alloy tubing and torn fibreglass Barry appeared from the wreckage, grinning from ear to ear, and announced: 'I've made history today. Nobody else has broken the landspeed record upside-down.'

Alas, neither had he. Although quicker by 4 miles-an-hour than the existing record for the standing quarter-kilometre, he would have had to make the run twice – once in each direction – for the record to be ratified. With his car in pieces that clearly was out of the question.

The bother of having to raise more cash and find new sponsors before he could try again was the least of the irrepressible Mr Bowles' problems, however.

'I'm a bit worried what my wife Jenny will say after all I've put her through these past few months,' said Barry gloomily.

Among the things he had already put the unfortunate Mrs Bowles through were: the loss of his job (with an insurance company, of all things); having to sell most of their furniture; and taking out a massive second mortgage on their home to raise funds for the car.

'I've been having a go at him to stop, but it's impossible.

This thing is like an addiction with him,' said Mrs Bowles.

Hard on the heels of passing her driving test, Christine Adam-czewska, 24, dashed off to the local registry office and got a marriage licence too. Said the breathless bride: 'It was certainly a nerve-racking day.'

Major row ahead

Police had to issue His 'n' Hers driving summonses after Jim and Janis Lewis took their little disagreement for a spin through the streets of Joplin, Missouri.

He told her to turn right, *she* told him to boil his head, *he* grabbed the steering wheel, and the *car* ended up in a grocery store after crashing through the window.

The couple were still arguing about it when the police arrived, so the judge was left to sort out the mess.

Track record

An awful lot of women drivers know the feeling. It's the first thing they say after the crash: 'Please don't let my husband know.'

It was precisely what Honni Blau said to police after bashing up the family Datsun.

But to keep the news from her husband would have required little short of another Watergate.

Mother of seven Honni was tootling past North London's busy Stamford Hill station when she lost control.

The car shot down an embankment, ploughed across a platform and ended up neatly straddling two busy railway lines.

A British Rail spokesman said: 'She's lucky to be alive. Trains come through every ten minutes.

'The whole thing has left everyone baffled. No-one can figure out how this woman managed to get the car across both tracks. It was a remarkable piece of driving, the sort only a woman could perform.'

When husband Ben heard the news he laughed so much it raised his blood pressure.

But Honni maintained: 'I'm a good driver – Ben's the lousy one.'

Oriental female seeks tall, slim, honest, responsible, caring, humorous, warm-hearted, cheerful, smart, lively, understanding, professional, successful bachelor, 28-35. Non-smoker. – **From the 'Friends Wanted' column of the** *Ruislip Focus*.

Just the ticket

When his wife told him she had taken two lovers, traffic warden Jaroslaw Lojko wreaked a terrible revenge.

He sent them parking tickets.

This caused considerable bafflement to the gents concerned, seeing as how they had been nowhere near the part of town specified on the tickets.

And after receiving half a dozen of the blasted things apiece, they asked Toronto city traffic authorities to explain themselves.

They in turn asked Jaroslaw to explain himself. How come, they queried, that you never stick the tickets under the wipers in the approved manner? Why do you always post them?

Elementary, said Jaroslaw. Every time he started writing out a ticket for the cars involved, their drivers appeared, got behind the wheel and skedaddled.

Hardly convinced by this explanation, the authorities probed even further. It all came out in court where Jaroslaw's pretty wife, Maria, said he was a man eaten up by jealousy. He constantly suspected her of having flings with every man she met.

It was all cruelly unfair, said Maria, for she was a model of wifely fidelity. However, just to shut the fool up, she confessed to the phoney affairs.

She hardly even knew the guys. One only hopes their wives believed Maria, even if Jaroslaw, on his way to a year in prison, probably didn't.

Old Wives' Tales

The hearts and flowers school of matrimony reckons that for a marriage to survive you've got to work at it, compromise and, above all, share things.

The happily married Rosalind Runcie, the concert pianist wife of the Archbishop of Canterbury, reports she and her husband have certainly adopted the sharing side of marriage.

Says Mrs R.: 'He falls asleep during my concerts; I fall asleep during his sermons.'

Old Wives' Tales

Spirited defence

The prosecution maintained it was murder plain and simple. No it wasn't, insisted Francisco Deas. It was an accident. The sort of thing that could happen to anyone.

There he had been, with the gun in his hand when BOOM! – didn't the blasted thing go off. And as the smoke cleared he perceived his young wife, Gleide, exiting pretty rapidly in the direction of Kingdom Come.

If the prosecution did not exactly sneer, 'Oh yeah? Pull the other one,' it was largely the tenor of their thoughts.

In his prison cell the much-doubted Francisco mused on his darkening future. What I need, he thought to himself, is a witness.

And just like that, the idea came to him.

'I know,' he said. 'Let's ask Gleide herself what happened.'

The Brazilian police, who have little experience of interviewing dead wives, left it all up to him. So the resourceful Francisco hired himself a medium and laid on a seance.

Before a silent throng of 100 independent spectators, the psychic rapped the table or whatever and in no time at all was rabbiting away to the late Gleide up there in Kingdom Come.

She, oh sweet forgiving woman, sent three spirit messages through the ether and lo and behold when the medium wrote them down, they were found to be in Gleide's own dear hand. PS: She also sent Francisco her love.

The crowd was agog. We're agog. Aren't you? Even more important, the Campo Grande jury was most agog. And after reading the messages, which roughly said Francisco was toying with the gun and suddenly it went BOOM! and . . . the jury discharged the 31-year-old widower almost as snappily as he had discharged the weapon.

Now there are some who doubt that Gleide ever said a thing to the medium; but then there are many others prepared to believe it. After all, say they, a woman always has to have the last word.

Jingle belles

Down in the grotto, where the fairy lights twinkled and the yuletide tunes tinkled away, Father Christmas was rapidly reaching the conclusion that this was indeed the season of goodwill to all. Well, to all women, anyway.

One after another, the ladies trooped in to tell him what they wanted from Santa Claus – a bit of the old ho ho ho.

Underneath the false whiskers Chris Christmas – and that, so help us, is his *real* name – was having a decidedly festive season.

Until Mother Christmas found out.

What with one thing and another, Margaret Christmas couldn't help but notice. Said she: 'I couldn't believe it when I saw a queue of women without children waiting to sit on his knee.

'And his beard was covered in lipstick.'

Thereafter women were barred from entering the grotto, unless accompanied by a child. And Margaret, 50, mounted guard at the Liskeard, Cornwall, pet shop in case 52-year-old Chris pulled any more Christmas crackers.

One of his fans, shopworker Debbie Bretherton, 23, enthused: 'Some of the girls popped in out of curiosity and Santa was so jolly we couldn't resist him.'

Not that Chris resisted much either. He cheerfully admitted: 'I don't discourage the girls. I've cuddled nearly a hundred.'

Ho ho ho indeed.

Gigantic bridal gown sale. – **Ad in the *Brentwood Advertiser*.**

I loved Lucy

'I haven't been tempted to get married again,' said Mr Harry Bidwell on the occasion of his 106th birthday. 'I am happier as a bachelor.'

Mr Bidwell first married at the age of 92, taking as a bride Lucy, 27 years his junior. But they broke up when he was 101 after constantly bickering over the housework.

Friends and neighbours

After 35 years of marriage, they split up. But there was never any real animosity between Sidney and Joan Boas and they remained on the chummiest of terms.

As was amply demonstrated when Sydney went hunting a retirement home.

He was enchanted by a two-centuries-old Georgian weatherboard cottage in a tranquil Kent village.

It's just what I want, he told the estate agent. Now, have you got anything else like that for my wife?

The enterprising agent quickly suggested the house next door and the couple seized on the idea.

Sydney, 61, a former computer engineer, said: 'We just couldn't live together. One thing is that I smoke which she can't stand.'

When he told Joan he was moving to the countryside, she wanted to go too.

Sidney added: 'We reckon it's the perfect situation. Friends have said to me why didn't I do that years ago.'

And estate agent Andrew Hyde said: 'Most people want to get as far away as possible from each other after a marriage break-up.

'But Mr and Mrs Boas are very happy about their new living arrangements.'

Fight to the death

The unpleasantness between the proverbial cat and dog was as nothing compared to the up-and-downers that Mary and Des Weindorf used to have.

For 21 years they rowed, taking breaks only to sleep, have babies where applicable or to kiss and make up in preparation for the next bout.

At length and after seven children Mary knocked it on the head. Off she went and got herself a divorce.

There followed 13 years of peace and quiet when each Weindorf sought but failed to find a new partner. So they married each other again.

And off they embarked on another marathon brawl, this time lasting all of 14 years before a second divorce. The general consensus of opinion at the time was: 'If he/she were the last man/woman on this earth I still wouldn't have anything to do with him/her.' Mutual, you might say.

The tranquil years rolled by and gradually took their toll of both ex-sparring partners. At 79 Des had to move into a Chicago nursing home.

Last year Mary, now 85, also became too frail to fend for herself. But when she tried to find a nursing home the only one around with any room was where Des had hung his hat.

With much trepidation the old lady entered the home. Next thing you know, Des started sending her prezzies and she started looking forward to them.

From that it was a short step back to the altar and their third marriage, and their umpteenth row.

Not that their children mind. They reckon the rows keep mom and pop fighting fit.

Said youngest daughter Sue: 'My mother had lost the will to live when she went into the home. She was in a wheelchair and was told she would never walk again.

'But she was able to walk down the aisle and now she is off the medication she had been on for 20 years. My father too is off all medication.'

Double bed

Widow Maria Vriniotis was much exercised to awake in the middle of the night and find a burglar sitting on the edge of her bed.

She was even more bemused when the man crawled in beside her and fell asleep.

Asked at the trial in Greece why it took her three hours to summon assistance, Maria explained: 'I was stunned. He looked so much like my husband who died two months ago, it left me in a daze. But when I realized my mistake I called the police.'

Pyjama game

After 44 years of *her* marriage, Doreen Collick finally came clean about her washday blues.

Every week throughout her married life she had hung a pair of her husband's pyjamas on the line. Sometimes it was a grey pair, sometimes a discreet blue and sometimes a rakish red.

But her 68-year-old husband, Richard, never wears the things. He sleeps absolutely stark naked.

Doreen confessed: 'If I didn't hang out the pyjamas then everyone would guess. And that would be embarrassing.'

Richard, of Plympton, Plymouth said by way of explanation: 'I stopped wearing pyjamas in 1937 when I joined the Navy.'

Added Doreen: 'I wash them in strict rotation and I've worn out dozens of pairs over the years.

'I even hang up his pyjamas to dry when we go on camping holidays. But he still doesn't wear them.'

Sheikh not stirred

Asked by some damn-fool reporter how he felt about the birth of his son, Sheikh Mohammed Abu-Zidon told Tel Aviv radio: 'You don't get excited any more.'

Presumably if you had three wives, 42 other children and

two more on the way, you wouldn't be dishing out the cigars either.

Wedding Day Blues

Those of our readers who are of a nervous disposition and who are about to wed should read no further. Kindly leave this page.

Have they gone? Good. Now we can tell you about all the terrible things that can go wrong on the day itself.

Best men lose the ring, airlines lose the luggage and bridegrooms lose their nerve. But those are only minor snags compared to some of the beauts we've got over the page.

And even if the day goes without a hitch will it be all right on the night? Don't bet on it. Joan Collins no less tells us what she and Peter Holm got up to on their honeymoon night – they fell asleep.

'Can you believe that?' she exclaims. 'Alexis fell asleep on her wedding night.'

Still, after three previous wedding nights we suppose one does become a bit blasé.

Wedding Day Blues

Maid of dishonour

Amply tooled up with boxes of Kleenex and polaroid cameras, the ladies of the congregation settled back to enjoy a good old traditional wedding.

For the courtship between Billy Paul Martin and Julianne Miller had been a traditional affair. At 17 she had been his girl next door. Now, eight years on, she was about to become his wife.

And what a fine bride she made as she glided down the aisle of the Simi Valley Episcopalian Church in California on the arm of her daddy.

Up in the ringside seats her mum gave a moist maternal beam that coupled pride and grief. The organist pulled out all the stops, the 260 guests murmured wonderingly of Julianne's beauty, her radiance, her dress. Oh, it was great stuff altogether.

Even Billy Paul himself felt the strings of his heart go zing, and considering the night he had just had, it was amazing he felt anything at all.

As Julianne finally drifted up to the altar, her maid of honour, Pamela Austin, gave her one of those 'you're my bestest friend in the whole world and I'm ever so happy for you' smiles.

It was somewhere around here that the ceremony broke with tradition. As the minister started to embark on the business Julianne whispered she wanted to say a few words to all and sundry. Right on, said the Rev, and she had the floor.

The bride turned first to her fond parents. Thank you for having me, said Julianne. Thank you for the years of love and understanding. Thank you for helping me with my wedding day.

By this time, as you can imagine, there wasn't a dry eye in the house.

Julianne in honeyed tones turned to the guests. Thank you for your loyalty, thank you for coming, thank you for all the wonderful gifts.

And she had a special word of gratitude for best pal Pamela.

'I would like to thank her,' Julianne said ever so sweetly, 'for sleeping with my groom last night.'

Gapes, gasps, pandemonium, consternation and all other hell broke loose. The ex-bride chose to miss the fun by storming out the door like a Spanish galleon with a stiff wind on its side.

Dad was left to pick up the pieces, and a heroic job he made of it. But once he pointed out there was no need to call off the wedding reception just because there was no wedding, and he had lashings of drink and food prepared, everyone calmed down.

Of course Julianne gave it the cold shoulder. As did Billy Paul. And Pamela deemed it would be less than fitting if she turned up to quaff the pink champagne.

Mum, Veronica Miller, despite everything, still in there pitching for her daughter, said: 'It came as a complete surprise to us all.

'Apparently the maid of honour took part in Billy's stag night the previous evening. It seems to have been a riotous affair.

'They got the boy drunk and before the wedding next morning one of his friends told our daughter what had happened.

'She and the boy have been sweethearts since their teens. It all seems so tragic that something like this should keep them apart.'

Billy Paul begged Julianne's mum and dad to get her to reconsider but she was having nothing more to do with the rascal.

Mrs Miller reported back: 'She is old-fashioned in that way.'

Now Julianne is looking for a new man. And when you come to think of it, a new best friend too.

Signing the register at a recent wedding the best man had difficulty in making the ball point pen work and was told to put his weight on it. He duly signed: 'John Smith (ten stone four pounds)'. – **From the parish magazine at Cawthorne, Yorkshire.**

Hymn and her

Asked by a Warwickshire vicar why they had chosen the hymn 'Sheep may safely graze' for their wedding service, the bride replied: 'Because we are both vegetarians.'

Arabian nightmare

She was romantic, playful, dewy-eyed; everything the ideal bride is supposed to be on the first night of her honeymoon.

71

The only snag was Bahira Tolba was supposed to be the groom.

And the real bride, Suad Shaheen, fled in tears when she discovered the man of her dreams was another woman.

Not only . . . but also – Bahira was already married, and the mother of two young children to boot.

When Cairo police investigated the case they found Bahira had rather a penchant for dressing herself up as a chap and making eyes at passing girls.

She also liked to pose as a wealthy jeweller, under the manly name of Mohamed Saleh. It was as such that she stole the heart of 20-year-old Suad.

But at the end of the whole sorry affair police threw the clerk at the registry office in the slammer.

They explained that he should have spotted Bahira's drag act and spared the bride's blushes.

Sacre cordon bleu

Had she beaten the child to death with a lucky horseshoe, there's not a court in the land that would have convicted her.

Instead, showing superhuman powers of self-control, bride Julie Loveridge muttered darkly under her breath and got on with the show.

The outrage came at that fraught moment in any wedding ceremony. The registrar was asking whether there was anyone present who knew of any reason why the two should not be joined in lawful matrimony and so on.

Suddenly a clear voice yelled out: 'Yes!'

As guests gazed at each other with a wild surmise, the voice added: 'She can't cook.'

Who could it be, this Egon Ronay of marriage wreckers? Why, it was none other than little Georgie, the bride's 13-year-old brother.

It was nearly five minutes before the Wisbech, Cambridgeshire, registrar could carry on with the ceremony, what with half the guests nearly having heart attacks and the rest laughing fit to bust.

Afterwards when Julie, 22, and William Besley were

declared man and wife, without any more jolly japes from the boy George, the bride's mother said: 'I thought she was going to faint.

'I could have killed George. She was very cross at the time but I know he didn't mean any harm and we all saw the funny side of it afterwards.'

Mrs Alder Loveridge added: 'But he's definitely wrong about Julie's cooking. She's never burnt a thing.'

Still, she might feel tempted to try: starting with George.

Own goal

Art designer Julie Honeymoon blew the whistle on footballer John Robson after just 24 hours of wedded bliss.

For 26-year-old John, once an apprentice with Fourth Division Darlington, had forgotten to mention his previous outings on to the matrimonial field.

Bride No. 1 was a 23-year-old salesgirl. John left her the day after the wedding to attend soccer trials, and never returned.

Bride No. 2 was 21-year-old nurse Susan Cowley. They wed in June 1984, but she walked out on him after three days when she discovered he was still married to wife No. 1.

Determined to make it a hat-trick, John then set out to woo Julie, and married her after a two-week whirlwind romance. That, too, was to prove disastrously short-lived.

Afterwards a repentant John, from Middlesborough, said: 'I know I've been a bit of a lad, but that's behind me. I really love Julie and want her back.'

Small change

It was only natural that a Manchester bride wanted her favourite hymn played as she tripped down the aisle, the tune in question being 'All things Bright and Beautiful'.

It was then pointed out to her that the second line runs: 'All creatures great and small.'

Further, it was pointed out that her groom was a great strapping fellow of 6ft 3ins, while she was only a smidgeon over 5ft 1in.

The bride-to-be rapidly changed her tune. Even so, she still managed to end up with something rather fitting – 'Love Divine All Loves Excelling'.

Here bums, they cried

News that the Rev William Spooner lives on – in spirit at least – reaches us from Berkshire. At a country wedding there a vicar pronounced the couple 'joyfully loined' in holy wedlock.

Oh happy, happy day.

Arms and the Woman

The catalogue of crimes that woman visits upon her poor unsuspecting spouse, and the armoury of weapons she brings to bear in the battle of the sexes, is, as all her victims know, wide-ranging, far-reaching and infinitely varied. Of course, the victim doesn't always need to be the husband, although he invariably ends up on the receiving end as well – like divorcee Dr John McElwey, whose ex-wife disliked the idea of his getting married again so much that she took up arms against his long-suffering bride-to-be by kidnapping her, hacking off her hair, covering her with tar and feathers and then throwing her on the city dump. Justifying her strange behaviour afterwards, the good doctor's ex wailed: 'It was justice for the bride. She was trying to take my husband away.' Still you can't help but feel that Dr John got off somewhat lightly when you consider what happened to some of the other victims whose sorry tales are recounted herein . . .

Arms and the Woman

Trouble down under

Here's one to fairly make the eyes water . . .

When he found himself another woman, Australian Leitu Fiso was fool enough to tell his current live-in girlfriend all about it.

Loonier still, he then went off to bed, leaving the heart-broken Vailnaila Louisi weeping bitter tears.

But soon her sorrow dried on her cheeks and the betrayed one felt the first stirrings of a terrible revenge. She picked up a knife . . .

Leitu didn't feel a thing, as he was fast asleep. On waking, rather sharpish we would imagine, he found himself bereft of his manhood and the foul Vailnaila waving a bloodied knife.

The night was only just beginning for Leitu.

In an apparent fit of remorse, Vailnaila dropped the knife and offered to drive her ex-lover and his ex-member both to hospital.

But when they made it to casualty, she managed to get her hands on the thing for the second time that evening. This time she secretly dumped it in a rubbish bin.

Luckily for Leitu and his new love, a nurse somehow found it and micro-surgeons at Sydney's Prince of Wales hospital toiled through the night to sew it on again.

But would it work? There was only one way to find out, and within a month doctors were advising him: 'Try it out on a prostitute.'

Leitu did. He duly reported back: 'The test was a success. It made me very happy, though I suffered some pain when he hit it.'

Meanwhile Vailnaila was in prison – the sex offenders' wing we hope – on charges of assault and grievous bodily harm. They don't come more grievous than that.

Leitu added: 'When it was cut off I thought I was going to die.'

The operation, he said, was little short of a miracle. 'I'm not a Christian but I really thanked God.'

The Annual meeting of the Ancient Order of Henpecked Husbands at Halifax, Yorkshire, was cancelled because none of the members was allowed to attend.

The French connection

Woken by his wife's futile attempts to kill him by wiring him up to the electricity supply, Rene Camembert, of Bobigny, Paris, leapt out of bed, grabbed a rifle, and shot her in the thigh.

When the couple duly appeared in court charged with trying to murder each other it was the French state electricity company that emerged as the unwitting and silent hero of this most unusual domestic drama.

It transpired that M. Camembert had woken up one morning to find his beloved standing over him wearing a pair

78

of rubber gloves and clutching an extension lead, one end of which had been attached to his head and the other to the mains supply. For good measure Mme. Camembert, a thorough woman, had placed a wet sheet over her husband's heart.

'I had hoped that the effect would be similar to that of an electric chair,' explained Mme. Camembert through her lawyer.

And so it would have been if the current had been the normal 220 volts.

The couple live, however, in one of the very few streets in Paris where Electricité de France, for reasons of economy, has retained the old 110-volt system.

Commented the magistrate: 'This case definitely has an element of the bizarre in it.'

Trigger happy

In the chilling wee small hours of the morning a frightened wife woke from a nightmare in a cold sweat.

She yearned for the security of her husband's arms – but he was out of town on a business trip.

So Barbara Osborne-Shaw settled for the next best thing. His small arms.

Leaping out of bed she grabbed her husband's loaded air gun and plunged back between the sheets with it by her side.

But no sooner that she had dropped off again than she had another nightmare, and as she tossed and turned she accidentally fired the gun, shooting herself in the knee.

Barbara, a nurse, ended the night in bed in the casualty ward at a Worthing, Sussex, hospital.

A sympathetic spokesman reported: 'It seems the lady took the gun to bed with her to feel a bit more secure after her nightmare. Unfortunately, it did not turn out too well.'

Hard to swallow

As every good housewife knows, a girl always tidies things away after a meal.

Diane Fellman apparently did not know, but then no-one is describing her as the ideal housewife.

Bored with looking after her invalid husband, she shot him, chopped him up and grilled the bits on her patio barbeque.

But she forgot to clean up afterwards, and was duly arrested when a neighbour spotted a man's jawbone in her back garden.

The 36-year-old hairdresser was jailed for life after prosecutor Richard Gardner told a San Jose, California, court: 'She's the coldest person I have ever met.'

The unrepentant Mrs F. even boasted of taking a nibble out of her late husband to see what he tasted like.

Despite having acted as foster parents to 47 children, Mr and Mrs Harry Hough of Leigh, Lancashire, were rejected by the Wigan Social Services Department as adoptive parents because their marriage was said to be free from rows, arguments and 'other negative experiences' which, the WSS contended, were essential ingredients to successful adoption . . .

Hard Luck Story

The bride wore handcuffs and the honeymoon wasn't half the fun it was supposed to be, what with the groom having to spend the night alone in a police cell.

Still, the unhappy couple were only asking for trouble when they set the date for Friday the 13th.

Bad luck abounded when the various in-laws suddenly took a violent dislike to each other and commenced to turn the reception into a rough house.

Police called to the newly-wed's Fulham, West London, council flat took appropriate action.

They arrested 13.

Family planning clink

After 12 years of marriage and their fortieth birthdays speeding towards them clippety-clop, Noel and Marie Murray felt it was high time they started raising a family.

The only problem was both were forced to lead a life of manifest chastity – as top-security prisoners in Limerick jail.

The husband-and-wife bank robbers maintained the Irish Government was breaching their constitutional rights by forbidding them their conjugal rights.

But the High Court ruled that prison security needs justified the love ban.

Another Irishman barred from enjoying a family was police officer Michael Reynolds. The Murrays did not refer to his case during their appeal.

He was, after all, the man they murdered during a bank raid.

Battle-axed

On the sound basis there is no fool like an old 'un, 78-year-old Alfonso Vedi swore a duel to the death when he heard his fiancée was seeing a younger man.

His rival, Liborio Amante, readily consented to the knife fight. But then Liborio – at 75 – was no chicken either.

At the appointed hour the grizzled warriors came face to face in the packed piazza of Agrigento, Sicily, where hot-blooded dingbats are not exactly unheard of.

Somewhere in the gawping throng was the femme fatale of the affair, Maria Zambito, a mere innocent of some 50 years.

Meanwhile the spectators were growing restive; this septuagenarian showdown was hardly the most rivetting spectacle since the Frazier–Ali bout.

For ten minutes on end, the old duffers contented themselves waving their knives about and saying awfully rude things to each other.

At last, in a quick one-two, both men struck. Alfonso copped a flesh shoulder wound, Liborio was holed in the trousers and leg.

The crowd shrugged its collective shoulders, turned on its heel and mooched off grumbling. As did the ungrateful Maria who refused to have anything to do with her bleeding boyfriends.

She sniffed: 'If they are stupid enough to fight over a woman, I don't want either.'

Ashes to ashes

Smoking, as the cigarette packets warn, can seriously damage your health.

Spaniard Justo Segui did not heed the warnings, which is partly the reason why all of a sudden he stopped smoking – and breathing.

But the main reason was he didn't heed his wife's warnings either.

Not that she was against smoking or anything like that. It was just she held the reasonable view that cigarette ash should be deposited in cigarette ash trays.

But Justo was basically a slob, who dumped his ash and his fag ends wherever he damn well liked. As you can imagine, this led to frequent heated exchanges between Mrs S. and her slovenly spouse.

Police called out after one particularly fierce barney found the inside of his home looking like open day at the crematorium.

It was ankle-deep in cigarette ash, the accumulation of years.

In the midst of it all lay the late, unlamented Justo, 61, beaten to death by his long-suffering wife and daughter.

Courting Disasters

Heavyweight champ Frank Bruno was fiercely parrying attacks on boxing as a killer sport.

The canvas ring, Frank claimed, was no more dangerous than any other sporting activity. And for the benefit of his Fleet Street interviewer he proceeded to list a string of deadly pursuits.

People get killed, Frank opined, playing rugby, running around and bashing into each other; they get killed motor racing, spinning around and crashing into each other. Jockeys get killed falling off horses. The list dragged on.

Then Frank delivered the uppercut: 'You can even get killed making love.'

A sudden hush fell on the interview. 'Making love?' someone repeated faintly.

'Yes,' said the triumphant champ. 'AIDS, you know, AIDS.'

Fortunately, as the following yarns reveal, there are much less disastrous ways of courting disaster.

Courting Disasters

Kiss and kin

She stooped to conquer when she knelt down to fill her jug at the village communal water tap.

A knot of tourists halted in silent appreciation of Anna-Maria's doe-eyed beauty and lissom figure. Among them was medical student Panayiotis Petrakis who appears to have gone on holiday leaving his brains behind.

For, rash youth, he dashed forward and kissed the lovely Anna-Maria on the cheek. Twice.

Now, in many parts of the world this sort of behaviour is likely to earn you a smack on the kisser; maybe even an embarrassing interview with the constabulary.

Not so in Mani, which is a village tucked away in the fold of some Greek mountain. There the citizens know precisely how to deal with violent desperadoes like P. Petrakis. They kill 'em.

And so within minutes of the incident, the wretched Romeo found himself fleeing for his life, pursued by an armed posse of hillmen.

In the lead we find Markos Kyvelos, 32, who had just happened to witness the dastardly assault on his sister's honour. Close behind come Anna's other big brothers, Yorgos and Savvas, with a mob of village toughies bringing up the rear.

It doesn't take long to corner their quarry in a dusty little alley where they leave him for dead, with four bullet holes spaced about his person.

At this point Panayiotis had his first spot of luck: he didn't die.

Moreover, his tourist mates were medical students too and they knew how to staunch wounds, apply tourniquets, all that sort of thing.

Panayiotis was the star witness at the subsequent trial of Markos, Yorgos and Savvas. It was a lengthy hearing, what with their lawyer insisting they had to shoot him to satisfy their sister's honour, and the prosecution saying rats to that.

85

After six weeks the three Kyvelos brothers went to jail for 15 years apiece for attempted murder.

As for little sister. She had fallen for the man whose kisses had landed her brothers in choky. Their love flourished in the dark corridors of the courthouse during recesses.

At the end of the trial, 18-year-old Anna-Maria announced their engagement, even though he should never have kissed her, she said.

But she added in all fairness: 'I also think my brothers were wrong to gun him down in the street.'

Petrakis, 21, who apparently had still not been reunited with his brains, enthused: 'The bullets were worth it, if only because they led me to discover the girl of my dreams and my future wife.'

And this man is going to be a doctor?

The views of Markos and Yorgos and Savvas are not available. Even if they were, we doubt if we'd be allowed to print them.

Dear Fred

You're not going to like this because I have returned your engagement ring to your sister Gladys. Knowing you so well I know you will wish me all the happiness when I tell you that I have married your father.

> *With all our love,*
> *Mum.*

– Letter to British Prisoner of War in Germany, 1943.

Necktie

Out there in the natural world the mating game ain't always that hunky dory either.

Spare a thought for the three male giraffes at Taipei zoo, left devastated when their much-loved lady giraffe upped and died.

In desperation the three became raving woofters and started necking with each other.

Zoo-keeper Chen Pao-chun, suitably mortified by the affair, promised to import females from Africa to break up the boys.

He added: 'The zoo is running out of explanations to tell children who ask us what the giraffes are up to.'

Then there was the zoo in Pretoria which became much exercised over the alarming shortage of sloths – there being only two in all of South Africa.

Happily one was a male and the other wasn't, so they put them together. And did they have lots of little slothettes? The hell they did. They were far too slothful for all this mating malarkey.

Not now, darling – I've got a headache.

At the other extreme is John Welsh's heron. It's not a real one, actually. It's made of plastic but it's life-size and life-like.

John forked out £12 to install it in his Crediton, Devon, garden in the fond hope it would scare off herons which had been breakfasting off his goldfish.

Herons, you see, are not supposed to invade each other's territory. But one did, and fell head-over-tail feathers in love with it.

Things got so bad that John took to hiding his decoy bird elsewhere in the garden but the heron always found it and stood around billing and cooing like nobody's business.

After some weeks of this nonsense without so much as a cheep from the decoy, the poor old heron gave up and flew off.

'But it was heartbroken,' said John.

And we'll take his word for it.

There is also the story of Rodney the goose who lived up to his species' reputation for folly by falling in love with a watering can.

His owner, Mrs Sylvia Court of Buckland Brewer, N. Devon, tried to set things straight by buying the booby a brace of beautiful lady geese.

To no avail. Rodney was nothing if not faithful and he stuck by the battered old watering can, despite his love's weird penchant of spitting on the herbaceous borders.

Tyred and emotional

The earth sure moved for both of them that night on Cedar Beach, not that Jeff Corwin and Lauri Zyburo enjoyed the experience.

There they were, cuddling under a counterpane of stars and a car rug, two young lovers, far from prying eyes amid the sand dunes.

Then a roaring great truck loomed over the horizon straight at them, and crushed them into the sand.

Later at a New York hospital, Jeff, with the tyre marks still etched on his face said: 'I saw the shadow of the truck out of the corner of my eye but it was too late to move.'

Both were able to dig themselves out and walk away. Their survival, said doctors, was 'nothing short of miraculous'.

Truck driver James Mason was pretty lucky too. Police said they would not be charging him.

Single electric blanket, hardly used, sale due to recent marriage. – **For sale ad in the *Newbury Advertiser*.**

Falling in love

Falling in love took on a whole new meaning for Allan and Pat Bellhaus when a leg of their double bed crashed through the floor and sent them sprawling on the carpet.

The incident, back in 1984, not only put an embarrassing end to their early morning bedroom romp, but had a furious Allan complaining to the town development corporation at Milton Keynes, where the couple live.

'Bedroom floors should be able to stand the strain, but ours is only made of chipboard,' complained a frustrated Allan.

Romeo, oh! Romeo . . .

Disturbed while visiting his girlfriend in the ground floor staff quarters of a Bournemouth Hotel, the young Lothario made a hasty exit by diving through what he thought was a window . . . and promptly disappeared down a 30-foot coal chute. He got a nasty bump on the head, but lived to love again.

The love bug

Only ten weeks after their first chance encounter, David West had his mind made up. The lovely Kim Paris was for him the perfect partner along life's ways.

There was, however, one slight snag. He hinted to her he had a Deep Dark Secret in the past. No, he couldn't tell her about it. It was just too awful.

West wasn't kidding either. He had shot dead in their beds the parents of a former girlfriend. It was the girl's idea but he was hoping for a slice of the £2 million estate.

Naturally this was not the sort of thing you would care to mention to a nice girl like Kim Paris. So every time the Deep Dark Secret came up, West tactfully changed the subject.

And then he proposed to her. 'It was love at first sight,' said he. 'Let's get married.'

Maybe, said Kim. But what about this secret?

Overcome by emotion, he told her everything. Even worse, he told her blouse.

And Kim's blouse, which concealed a tiny radio bug, relayed all this back to a brace of detectives, waiting in a nearby car.

Kim listened to all the gory details, letting West get it off his chest and on to hers. And then she asked him to stop his car because she wanted to buy cigarettes.

The love-smitten killer was still waiting for her to return when the officers moved in and carted him off to prison in Houston, Texas.

It was only later the 28-year-old delivery man learned that the love of his life was a private detective, hired by the family of the victims.

Kim, 23, got to meet him by knocking on his door one night and asking after some fictitious character. Blushing prettily when told she had made a mistake, she asked West if she could use his phone.

One thing led to another and that very same night he took her out for a drink. After that they met three or four times a week.

Kim later revealed: 'I kept dancing around the subject of

sex. Actually it wasn't that hard – he fancies himself as an intellectual.'

Her boss, Clyde Wilson, said: 'West certainly wasn't going to spill the beans to me or to any of my men. It seemed like a logical thing to do to bring a girl into the case to win his confidence.'

A Houston detective said admiringly: 'It was a gambit any detective story buff could have spotted a mile away. But this kid made it work.'

Sailor beware

She would be the first to admit it, Janet Anderson is the sort of girl who likes to paddle her own canoe.

But husband Torben is the sort of guy who can't resist sticking his oar in.

And they weren't long married when Janet mutinied and kicked him off her 27ft Bermuda sloop.

She ordered Torben to bob along in her wake on his own 31ft boat and come abroad only when she was at anchor for the night.

Welsh-born Janet, who met Torben sailing off the Costa Brava, said: 'Right from the start we realized we couldn't live together. He didn't want to be part of my crew and he started running things. I quickly told him I was the captain of my own ship.'

But she and Torben are still the best of mates, Janet insists.

She added: 'However far apart we drift, we know we are committed to each other and always come together in the end.

'We just have trouble sailing together, not sleeping together.'

Crimes of Passion

The true grand *crime passionel* is almost a thing of the past. Long gone are the days when Grandma shivered at the dastardly deeds of Dr Crippen who bumped off his wife for love of another woman; gone too are the days when dad quivered at the exploits of Ruth Ellis who drilled a hole through her boyfriend for loving another woman.

Nowadays it's the sin of passion which grabs the headlines. Who's playing footsie with whom, is the cry of the masses.

And it's surprising the undercover stories that emerge. Even that pillar of the moral majority, Ronald Reagan, has had his lapses.

One imagines a delicate blush suffuses his cheeks when he recalls the circumstances of his marriage to Nancy, the occasion being somewhat rushed on account of his bride being a couple of months pregnant at the time. Still, it all goes to show that passion lives on anyway.

Crimes of Passion

Dr Strangelove

Lesser women resort to lonely hearts clubs or placing discreet ads in the personal column.

But there was none of this namby-pamby stuff for frustrated spinster Dr Rochelle Konits.

She put out a contract to have the man of her dreams kidnapped and delivered to her home in a hypnotic trance.

'I'm not going to hurt him,' she told her hired henchmen. 'I'm going to kill him with love.'

Sadly for the 41-year-old general practitioner, the kidnappers were from the Nassau County District Attorney's office.

She ended up charged with conspiracy and supplying the undercover agents with a drug, one tablet of which can knock anyone out for up to five hours.

The agents said she promised them $500 if they snatched the middle-aged Manhattan doctor with whom she once had an affair.

Codswallop

The judge rejected a petition by 50-year-old Mrs Roberts alleging cruelty.

Among her allegations was that, 20 years ago, her husband, a shipwright, had slapped her round the face with a wet fish.

The judge said: 'If one slap with a wet fish in 20 years of marriage is cruel – and I don't consider that it is – then that cruelty has, in any case, been forgiven.'

Love-in-a-mist

It was meant to be one of those steamy nights of passion which red hot Latin lovers go in for.

Unfortunately it was nowhere near steamy enough, which was why a couple of teenagers ended up before a Turin court, accused of offending public morals.

They had been caught at it in a parked car, and a policeman, who surely should have had better things to do, was able to observe their antics.

The Italian Supreme Court later upheld the magistrate's decision, but ruled it's perfectly OK to romp around in a car in a public place *provided the windows are steamed up*.

And when they were nabbed, the couple's windows had not yet misted over.

Incidentally, the lovers appear to have been a pair of extra-ordinarily gifted contortionists. They were found disporting themselves in the back of a Fiat 500.

Date with death

Life apart was even worse for Christian and Nicole Granier than the days they used to spend together arguing and fighting.

So much so that the couple would meet frequently to reminisce over old times and even, on occasions, discuss the possibility of a reconciliation.

Then, one day, Christian spotted the lovely Nicole in a discotheque drinking with a male friend. So enraged was he that he went home to fetch his hunting rifle, followed Nicole to the police station at Castelnaudary, in Southern France, and shot her dead.

As he languished in prison, her death on his conscience and a murder rap hanging over his head, his friend, named only as Jose, told police: 'I hardly knew Nicole and we had only gone out for a drink because we were both lonely.'

Then he revealed that the topic of the conversation in which they had been so earnestly engaged when Christian confronted them was . . . none other than Christian himself.

Said Jose: 'The craziest thing was that she had just decided to go back with him.'

Ding dong dinner

Lest anyone got the wrong impression about him, Andrew Wilson was at pains to point out: 'I'm not a chauvinist.'

'But,' he added, 'I do like the more traditional role of the wife – cooking the meals, keeping the place clean, and a little cuddle.'

Sadly, his girlfriend, Linda Willoughby, held different views on where a woman ought to be.

And so it happened that bricklayer Andrew came back from a hard day's work to find a singular absence of either Linda or a hot meal. She was down at the pub.

Feeling hard done by, he set about preparing his own solitary dinner. Moreover he made some for his errant partner.

And, packing her sausages, chips and beans in a plastic bag, he breezed down to the pub where he gave Linda her dinner – all over her head.

The sorry affair ended at Dunstable, Beds, magistrates' court where Andrew was given a conditional discharge after admitting causing actual bodily harm.

The court heard he had later belted Linda with a chunk of wood after she threw a brick through his window.

After the case Andrew explained: 'I work very hard all day and all I want to do when I get home is sit down, have a cup of coffee, a read of my paper and my meal.

'Linda was just winding me up. At one time she used to say she hated the pub but then for the last two weeks she was down there at opening time without a thought for me.

'Since this has all happened, Linda has left for good but we are still on amicable terms.'

Give your wife a treat. Leave home at the weekends. – **Hotel advert in the *Lytham St. Anne's Express*.**

Dog in the manger

She was an air hostess but there was nothing flighty about her. Pity the same could not be said of him.

The first time they met, in a Mexico City coffee bar, Maria Vasquez thought Jose Martinez was the greatest thing since chilli peppers. He liked the look of her too.

As the handsome but jobless barman was temporarily out of luck, 26-year-old Maria invited him to move in with her.

Between flights, her apartment became a cosy little love-nest. Maria nursed dreams of becoming Mrs Martinez ere long. Jose was not particularly bothered but wisely didn't say anything about it.

For the apartment – although Maria was blissfully ignorant of it – had been turned into a passion pad. Every time she got on a plane, he got on the phone and rang another of his many girlfriends: 'Hey, Juanita . . .'

Then surprise, surprise, one day Maria came home unexpectedly to find the sheets crumpled and a pervading perfume which was not her own upon the pillow.

After a woefully inadequate lie or two, Jose finally confessed yes, he had been with another.

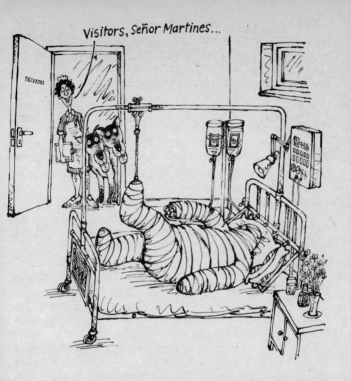

Visitors, Señor Martines...

But it was just because he was so lonely. It would never happen again, never ever, he swore.

Maria forgave him, even if she didn't believe him. And next time she took to the skies she had a private eye shadowing Jose.

On her return a fortnight later a sad dossier greeted her. Some four women had been to the flat in her absence. Jose had not spent a single night alone, the detectives reported.

Maria acted as if everything was still lovey-dovey and there followed four days and nights of hugs and kisses. On the last evening, before her next flight, they even dallied holding hands over a romantic dinner. Jose slept innocent as a babe that night.

In the morning he drove Maria to the airport, they kissed goodbye, she went off into the wide blue yonder and he went off like a rocket to the apartment.

But when he opened the door he found the place already occupied and the new tenants were distinctly unfriendly.

Neighbours heard his screams floors away. They got there in time to save him, but only just.

As the police later said: 'Two Alsatians had nearly savaged him to death. He was barely recognizable as a human being.

'He has had more than 100 stitches in his face, neck and head and he can hardly walk. No woman will ever look at him again.'

When Maria landed she went to the police and readily owned up to hiring Jose's attackers from a firm whose speciality is training savage dogs. She booked them over the phone that night of the romantic dinner.

She said: 'I could have tolerated him being lazy, but not having a string of women behind my back. My ego just wouldn't allow that.

'He insulted me and I just wanted to kill him.'

But in prison, awaiting trial on an attempted murder rap, Maria changed her mind.

She sent the much-embroidered Jose a bouquet of flowers and a get-well card inscribed 'with love'.

Oh, that's all right then.

Blooming nuisance

Julien Klasha said it with flowers when he sent a pot of May Day blooms to his sweetheart in Lyons.

But another suitor said it even better, by giving the mademoiselle a much bigger bunch.

Julien had the last say when he cornered his rival and promptly bumped him off.

Now Julien is serving an 18-year prison sentence and doesn't care a hoot who sends her flowers.

Indian love cell

Beauty, as they say, is in the eye of the beholder.

Well, by all accounts Dr Madhavan's young wife is a stunning beauty, but he's damned if he's going to let anyone behold her.

Indeed, the good doctor, when last heard of, was building a windowless prison cell to house his jewel.

Radha, for such is her name, is to be locked up in it 24 hours a day, except for those moments when he takes her out to have a good dekko at her or whatever.

Lest anyone think him an unfeeling man, Dr Madhavan is also constructing an adjoining bathroom where Radha can go and admire herself.

He has engaged the services of a retired copper to stand guard outside his home in the town of Kroor in India's Kerala province.

The cell, we are told, is to measure six feet square. It will be dark, to preserve Radha's delicate complexion, but he has thoughtfully included a ventilator, to preserve her life.

It is not the first time the good doctor has shown remarkable solicitude for her welfare. He has twice performed abortions to keep her in shape.

However, not everyone is touched by 42-year-old Madhavan's benevolence. Radha's big sister, Mrs Solly Idamruku, wants him locked up instead.

But police say the 20-year-old black hole beauty refuses to bring charges.

Berk and her

The little green god feasted nightly in the heart of James Wiles. For three solid years he nurtured the monster, saving all his money so it could carry out its fell intention.

When he had amassed some £2,000, Wiles deemed the moment was right.

The little green god did not want much, only the unconscious body of Doris, the former Mrs Wiles.

Wiles himself did not want someone to kill her for him. Oh

101

dear me no. That would have been no fun at all.

He wanted to do the killing, with his very own tie. But first he had to have her brought to him.

With a roll of banknotes in his pocket, he sought out two ruffians in a London East End pub and explained his requirements.

The body snatchers demanded £1,000 up front and a photograph of Mrs Wiles so they got the right woman. Hands were shook, glasses were raised and that was that.

On the morning arranged, the two kidnappers presented themselves at the door of Wiles' flat, saying Doris was unconscious downstairs and could they please have the other £1,000.

He handed over the money and urged his cronies to carry Doris to him. O.K., said they, just wait here a moment.

Wiles waited . . . and he waited . . . and after waiting round a bit more he thought he had better see what was going on. But when he went downstairs no trace of the villains could he find. Even more to the point, there was no trace of Doris either, conscious or otherwise.

Full of a seething indignation, Wiles stormed off to the cop shop to tell the Law all about these hitmen who had reneged on the contract.

As it was later recalled at the Old Bailey, he was so enraged he didn't stop to consider the consequences of what he was saying.

And pretty unpleasant those consequences were – five years in prison for incitement to kidnap. But of the kidnappers and his money never more was heard.

Equal Rites

The theory of marriage is both partners are equal. The practice is, as ever, some are more equal than others.

What better example than our very own Queen and, of course, Prince Philip.

On the eve of their visit to Nepal, the citizens of that high-rise country went hither and thither sticking up bunting and a whopping great banner that proclaimed: 'God Bless The Queen.'

Rather late in the day one of the organizers realized there was no similar salutation to Her Majesty's loyal husband. So a courier was dispatched to even the score.

He duly added a banner: 'God Help Prince Philip.'

Equal Rites

Vital statistics

If you want to live long enough to qualify for a basket of fruit and a congratulatory telegram from Her Majesty, get married.

But only if you're a man.

If you're a woman with the same life long ambition, for heaven's sake don't marry him.

Spinsters have a better chance than wives of celebrating their 100th birthdays. But bachelors are less likely than husbands to clock up the ton, according to a survey of 100 centenarians.

Mind you, of Britain's 3,000 century makers, only one in five is a man anyway. But then the centenarians polled did say that the secret of longevity is to avoid stress.

More vital statistics

Just in case you ever thought of defecting, it ain't all vodka and skittles for Russia's wedded comrades either.

Pravda reveals that a big bugbear in the life of Ivan and Olga is the shopping. Or rather, the shopping queues.

The Moscow newspaper reckons Russians spend 37 billion hours a year standing in line – that works out at 190 hours for every man and woman.

It is also a major factor in the break up of many marriages. Another complaint is that once they get inside the shops, they still can't buy the things they need.

There is, for instance, a perennial shortage of household cleaning appliances, like carpet sweepers; which is maybe just as well, seeing as there's a shortage of carpets too.

Meanwhile Americans have found a novel way of staying together – by living apart.

Around 1 million couples have commuter marriages, with husbands and wives living and working in different towns.

The only time they get together is at weekends or the holidays when they make up for all they've missed.

Much to the astonishment of marriage-ologists, absence really does make the heart grow fonder. The divorce rate among commuter couples is only one in ten.

Among us decent folks it's one in two.

My own wife, as some people know, had a lot of children – eight, if I remember rightly. – **Lord Longford in a House of Lords debate on women in public life.**

Tug-of-woof

There was no denying that he had big, melting brown eyes; nor that he brimmed over with affection and gentleness.

There was no denying either that he was a dog.

Still, to Alfred and Margaret Kerr, the dog, Turbo, might just as well have been a darlin' blue-eyed baby boy.

So when it came to pass that Alfred and Margaret parted,

neither wanted to give up custody of the beloved barker.

Indeed, the couple threatened to take their case to the House of Lords, and they might even yet have been arguing the toss, had Turbo not solved the wrangle himself . . .

He died.

Till death us do part

If you think married womankind has it tough here, spare a thought for those unfortunate souls who don't even have the benefit of the law on their side.

Like 18-year-old Narges Jabari, of Beshahr, in Northern Iran, who was executed by firing squad after an Islamic Revolutionary Court found her guilty of adultery.

Her 32-year-old lover was not so unlucky. He got off with 100 lashes on the grounds that, as he was single, his crime was less serious.

'The difference between the severity of the sentences was due to the fact that the woman was married,' said a court official by way of explanation.

Eye for an eye

Mind you, it's not entirely a man's world, even under the mad Mullahs.

For another court there gave permission for wronged wife Maryam Zavarei to blind her husband with a pair of scissors.

In what was literally an eye-for-eye judgment, the judge ruled that the wife, who had herself been blinded by her jealous husband, was not only free to seek retribution, but could even choose the method of its execution. She chose scissors.

Maryam, the court was told, had been driven out into the desert by her husband and held down by two men while he gouged her eyes out with a knife.

Justifying the 'cruel and inhuman' sentence, a court official explained that it was common practice in Iran to allow victims – or, in the case of murder, the victims' relatives – to select the punishment to fit the crime, adding that under Islamic law, 'it is normal for a thief to have a hand cut off, and a woman guilty of adultery to be stoned to death.'

Wedlocked

Jailbird lovebirds Patricia Watts and Len Saffley were finally allowed to wed in prison in 1984 after a long legal battle against Missouri authorities.

But they were barred from setting up home in the same cell at the State Pen.

Sanctioning the wedding Judge Howard Sachs said: 'Even prisoners have the right to make their own mistakes.'

Swiss role

Lest you think the Swiss are unromantic sorts, who keep their hearts locked up in bank vaults, along with their alpenstocks and shares, we recount the following yarn.

Billowing out of his Zurich courtroom, divorce judge Lutz Stamm came upon Rolf Meyer weeping bitter tears.

The judge, who had just granted Frau Meyer a divorce, tried to console the suddenly single Rolf.

'Oh, it's not the marriage,' explained the grieving ex-husband. 'It's the dog.'

As Judge Stamm listened sympathetically, Rolf spoke of his happy days with Ali, the pair's pet cocker spaniel. Rolf wept. The judge murmured platitudes and went on his way.

But the very next day Rolf got a call from a local kennels. There was a pedigree spaniel puppy awaiting him, would he please come and collect it.

A gentleman who would not give his name had selected and paid for the dog. What did he look like? Yes, you've got it. He was a dead ringer for Judge Stamm.

Altogether. now . . . Aaaaahhhh!

And further proof that at heart the Swiss are a nation of old softies: Only last year they voted to allow their womenfolk to open bank accounts and go to work without their husbands' permission.

State of the union

So now you know why they call it Virginia.

In the American state of that name it is not merely immoral to dip your toe in the water afore your wedding day – it's also downright illegal.

It's been that way since 1860. Heaven knows what they used to get up to in the good old days before then, but whatever it was, the State legislature wanted none of it.

And so was born the infamous 'Fornication Statute' which outlawed any pre-marital hanky panky.

This year an unmarried couple who desperately want to but aren't allowed to failed in their bid to have the killjoy rule killed off.

A Federal appeals court found that as they had not been prosecuted there was no need to change the law.

Whereupon the couple's indignant lawyer, Michael Morchower, said his unnamed clients would go on living with each other, but in a state of utmost chastity.

They were frightened they might end up on a morals rap if they started sharing the same duvet, he claimed.

Despite all this, the State tourist board still trumpets its motto: 'Virginia is for lovers.'

Name the day

It's not that he's an ardent women's libber or anything, but an Ecclesfield, Yorks, electrician opted to take his bride's surname on marriage.

'I didn't mind Brian's name but he never liked it,' said wife Mrs Sandra Denial.

'I've taken a lot of ribbing over the years because of it. When we married it seemed a good time to change it once and for all,' said the erstwhile Mr Tricklebank.

Mature, sincere, serious Irishman has an unfurnished apartment in Torreguadiaro. Will share same with mature, serious lady with her own furniture. – **From the matchmaker column of** *Lookout*, **an English language magazine in southern Spain.**

Love story

Franjo Saraga wanted to watch a television discussion on the Brussels football disaster. His wife, Barica, didn't, and tried to switch over to the American film *Love Story*.

The 56-year-old Yugoslav won the argument – he strangled his 45-year-old wife. Police later arrested him and charged him with murder.

That Was No Lady

There you are, down the King's Head enjoying a quiet birthday drink with your mates when all of a sudden this nun comes up to you and before you can say Hail Mary whips off her habit to reveal all the naughty bits.

You've just been caught by a kissagram.

The girls who ply this trade come in all shapes and disguises – the French Maid model (complete with feather duster), the WPC, the Lovely Rita meter maid.

Now there's a new version on the market. The Sara Keaysagram. Remember her? Cecil Parkinson, that most upright of Tory Ministers would rather not, but there you are.

This one comes in country tweeds, looks about eight months pregnant, bangs on your door and utters the immortal line: 'I have bad news . . .'

That Was No Lady

Out of touch

Team manager Klaus Winter dearly loved his football. Not so his blonde wife, Ute. She passionately loved his footballers . . . all of 'em.

How she thrilled to the skills of the strikers, how she whooped at the ways of the wingers, how she gasped at the grasp of the goalie. And that was only in bed.

How she ever managed time for it, heaven only knows. But the lovely Ute had affairs with 28 of her husband's players.

Of course that figure does include members of the reserves and Old Boys' side.

Klaus's first intimation that his wife was straying offside came when he found her in bed with his star forward.

Next he chanced upon Ute in the arms of the outside-left, in the clubhouse to boot.

Klaus contented himself with giving them a talk on team spirit. The game's the thing, all that sort of guff. Naturally Ute didn't take a blind bit of notice.

Before long the goalie's name had joined the list of those who had let the side and their trousers down. He was caught well out of his spot, making love to Ute in the back of a car.

Hard on his heels came a mid-field star, found taking a dive with the boss's wife in her lounge.

Men of a more suspicious nature, your Othellos of this world, might by now have figured out that Ute was doing more scoring than the entire first team. Not old Klaus.

He didn't know until his best friend told him and it was only with the greatest reluctance that he filed for divorce.

As he told a court in Mainz, West Germany: 'I kept quiet about her earlier affairs because I didn't want scandal for my club. It was my life.'

No denying that, said Ute, adding: 'All I wanted was a little tenderness. Klaus gave all his time to the club. I was lonely.'

The judge, clearly a man who understands just how lonely a girl can get, ordered Klaus to pay her a £25,000 lump sum plus £5,000 a year maintenance.

Too much, said the scandalized husband. 'I am being persecuted by the men who slept with my wife. They have warned me to keep my mouth shut . . . or else.'

'I am now hiding out in another town with a secret telephone number because I'm afraid they will take their revenge. My nerves are in shreds. I can't work.'

As for 27-year-old Ute: 'I've heard she's working in a bar and has lots of men friends.'

Get away!

LATEST SCORE: Klaus is writing a book to raise the maintenance cash. Its title: *Football Fouls*.

Hand-me-downs

An Alton, Illinois, housewife was so outraged by her husband's dress sense that she got a divorce. Mind you, he was a raging transvestite.

She had the last biting comment on his taste in frocks when she died, leaving him not a penny of her £68,000 will, but all her old dresses.

Her lawyer explained: 'It was a facetious act. Her husband liked dressing up in women's clothing and she wasn't too happy about it. This was the last laugh for her.'

To bee or not to bee

The three wives of a Brazilian polygamist dreamed up a dreadful revenge on the Don Juan.

It was like a gruesome version of *The Sting*; or maybe something out of a bad bee movie.

They lured him to a Sao Paulo hotel room and locked him in with a swarm of killer bees for company.

He smashed down the door but dropped dead in the car park, his body covered in stings.

The three furies were all convicted of manslaugher.

Hot and bothered

Like any other poor soul who has the misfortune to work nights, Giacomo Franchi had to put up with an awful lot of rabbit from his ever-loving wife.

So one night when the machine in his Naples factory broke down, he dashed off home early.

This will give Maria a nice surprise, thought he.

As he let himself into their flat, he carolled: 'It's all right, it's only me.'

Maria, snug between the sheets, mumbled a drowsy: 'Hello.'

Hot from hurrying home, Giacomo flung open the window, saying: 'This room needs fresh air.'

Whereupon there was a howl of terror, followed rapidly by a ghastly thud on the pavement two floors below.

'Oh, my god! You've killed him,' said Maria sitting up in bed.

For which unwise and inaccurate observation she earned a couple of black eyes. Her lover, Sandro Merlino, was rather worse off, though not as badly as Maria's initial assessment indicated.

Said Giacomo with grim satisfaction: 'With two broken legs he has had his punishment for now.'

The couple have since divorced.

WEDDING? Book now. Two Black Princesses for Weddings.
– Ad in the *Lymington Times*.

Dr who

The way Sandra Peterson saw it, her husband was just like any other red-blooded male. She certainly had no complaints on that score.

However, her six-year-old marriage had otherwise lost its sparkle and she wanted a divorce on the grounds that it was beyond repair.

Sandra got her parting all right, but only because a London divorce court judge ruled that her husband was *not* as other men.

For starters, he was a woman.

He entered this world as a bouncing baby girl, known to her mum and dad as Wendy Patricia.

It mattered not to the court that 20-odd years later she had a sex change operation and switched the name to Edward.

Judge Sir Jonathan Clarke dished it out straight: 'The law as I see it is clear – that a person's sex is determined effectively and for all time at birth.'

And without further ado he declared the marriage had never existed.

Former nurse Sandra emerged from the hearing a perplexed woman. She recalled how she met handsome psychiatrist Edward when both were working in the same hospital.

They fell in love and set up home together as man and wife, even though he told her all about his days as a Wendy.

Said Sandra: 'Our love life was satisfactory. It was a typical doctor-nurse relationship, I suppose.'

The sex swop op mattered not one whit.

'I was marrying the man and what went on before was a different world,' she added. 'He's as masculine as the next man, so it wouldn't have mattered to me if he had come from another planet.'

The nullity decree left Sandra with one headache: she had to explain to her 15-year-old son from a previous marriage that his step-dad was a woman, in the law's eyes anyway.

As she set off home to break things gently to the lad – who knew nothing of the sex-change – Sandra said with considerable justification: 'It has been a very harrowing day, to say the least.'

Made of the mountains

Maybe it's a sorry reflection on the morals of modern wives or maybe it's just because Welsh mountain farmers are more suspicious than most . . .

Blacksmith Emyr Jones reports he is doing a brisk trade in chastity belts. He said: 'It's true that some were given to people as presents. But that's all I'm saying.'

Equally reluctant to discuss the belts was Lampeter landlady Mrs Joy Patterson who hung one, adorned with scarlet knickers, above the bar of the King's Head Hotel.

Said she: 'There's nothing I want to say about it.'

Viewers in Houston, Texas, were treated to a TV commercial showing a slinky woman shimmering through the trees in a diaphonous gown and urging sweethearts: 'This Valentine's Day, give your lover a plastic surgery voucher . . .'

Road to the grave

Mrs Ruth Robinson was fat in the same way as Switzerland is hilly; that is to say spectacularly so.

Even the funeral of her dear husband was not enough to lure the mountainous Ruth out in public where she felt she would be seen as a figure of fun.

Instead she squeezed into the car and paid her last respects to the late Mr Robinson through the tinted window of a drive-in funeral parlour.

Tasteless? The Florida undertakers involved don't think so. A spokesman defended the practice thus: 'Mourners don't have to worry about their appearance or showing grief.'

Till Divorce Us Do Part

Put away your hankies, for this is no collection of unhappy-ever-after stories. Truth to tell, divorce can be even more fun than marriage.

Just ask Zsa Zsa Gabor who has more ex-husbands than you could shake a stick at. Even as you read this she's probably hunting down another one.

As she says: 'I am a wonderful housekeeper. Every time I get a divorce I keep the house.'

Now she's got more homes than Barratt's.

Others too have found that divorce, like marriage, is a decidedly mixed blessing . . .

Till Divorce Us Do Part

For richer, for poorer

While she was married to the guy, Nancy Radzik could see nothing good in her mate, John.

For starters, he was only a bricklayer and he certainly wasn't making a pile. Come every payday, she would tear open his wage packet and sneer at the pitiful contents.

'Is that all you can earn?' she would mock. 'It's not enough for one to live on, let alone two.'

This said, she would hand the hapless John his pocket money and, would you believe it, the no-good would blow most of that on lottery tickets.

After several years of this palaver, Nancy found herself a smart cookie salesman on a big salary and divorced 35-year-old John.

For all of 30 days the new Mrs Nancy Anderson was blissfully happy. Life was rich indeed, with money in the bank and a fistful of credit cards. Who could ask for more?

Well she certainly did when she heard that John's number had finally come up and he had won himself a million dollars in a lottery.

Naturally he told her to go play with the traffic when she demanded a piece of the action. But Nancy was a hard woman and she took John to court seeking compensation for all those years when he was blowing his pocket money on lottery tickets.

As his lawyer noted: 'She's remarried, she's got their house, she works and earns a pretty good living. According to her, when he was buying the lottery tickets he wasn't being a very nice man. But boy, suddenly he wins.'

Judge Howard Jones took the same view and he told the million dollar Massachusetts brickie to keep 'every single dollar'.

A housewife fed up with her lawyer husband always cross-examining her and the children petitioned for divorce on grounds of mental cruelty. She got her decree – but only after he had a last

123

fling at cross-examining her in the London divorce hearing.

Who's sari now

More sensitive men might have taken the hint years ago. Not the incorrigible Udaynath Dakhnaray.

His first bride walked out on him in 1949 and never bothered to return.

Was he dismayed? Did he change his deodorant? Did he stop wearing his socks in bed? Who knows?

But what he definitely did do was pledge himself to a life of polygamy, presumably as some sort of revenge upon the entire female sex.

When last heard of the wealthy 61-year-old landowner had just carried bride No. 89 across the threshold of his home in the Eastern Indian state of Orissa.

But he's still no great shakes as a husband. Of the 88 previous Mrs Dakhnarays, 58 fled the marital coop and four more will be following suit any day now.

The other 26? They've all gone to that great divorce court in the sky.

Post haste

'It was my wedding anniversary,' explained Mrs Saida Zeinab, wife of a Cairo merchant.

'Expecting a letter of congratulations from the government I opened the official envelope addressed to myself with happy anticipation. Imagine my surprise when I found it contained my certificate of divorce. What is more, the certificate was dated from six months ago.'

Asked why he had failed to tell his wife that he had divorced her, but continued to live with her, Mr Zeinab, who was charged with living with Mrs Zeinab under false pretences, said it had been done in a rush and he had forgotten all about it.

Hans off

Fritz Koch was the perfect husband – everybody told his pretty, 27-year-old wife Bettina so.

He adored her and their baby son Karl, and made sure they never wanted for anything.

For the 28-year-old night-shift sheet metalworker from Luben, in East Germany, that didn't just mean doing his best at work. He also toiled long and hard at home, expressing his love for his family in every way he could.

Cutting his daytime sleep short, he worked hard to make things easy for Bettina on the domestic front.

He did the shopping, cooking and washing-up, cleaned their apartment, and took care of the family laundry and ironing.

Not only that, he also bathed and fed little Karl, and even changed his nappies.

The upshot of all this, of course, was that poor Bettina was left with nothing to do. And that led them to the divorce court.

'He made me feel useless,' Frau Koch explained to the perplexed judge when she appeared before him to explain why she wanted to end their two-year-old marriage.

'At first I thought it was great to have such a considerate man as a husband. My girlfriends told me I had an angel of a man,' she told the judge. But, she went on, 'gradually it all got too much. He gave me an outsize inferiority complex.'

The judge took her point, explaining as he granted her a divorce: 'The husband harmed her personality.'

But the story of the perfect husband that millions of other women would love to have was not yet over. When last heard of Fritz and Bettina were still arguing about who would get custody of baby Karl. 'I still want to change his nappies,' explained Fritz.

Announcing her third divorce from her husband, Alfred, Mrs Margaret Mitchell, 53, of Basingstoke, Hants, explained: 'Things just didn't work out.'

Checkpoint Charlie

East German Joachim Matz braved bullets, mines and the other colourful impedimenta of the city limits when he legged it over the Berlin Wall.

Once safely ensconced in the West, he thought to himself: this is the life, I bet old Heide would love it too – Heide being his ex-wife.

So he wrote impassioned letters to the Communist authorities, begging them to let her join him. Months passed and his letters went unanswered but Joachim refused to give up.

He bought himself a cage, set it up at Checkpoint Charlie, crawled inside and staged a sole but spectacular protest against the rotten heartless Commies.

It was only then that someone thought it worthwhile to canvass Heide's opinions on the subject.

And she announced: 'I'm staying here. I don't want to see him again. It was a bad marriage and I'm glad I'm divorced.'

Joachim crawled right back out of his cage and returned to his lonely freedom.

After being carried into court on a stretcher terminally ill Mrs Earlano Wright, 62, of Fort Worth, Texas, assured the judge that she was 'absolutely sure' she wanted a divorce from her husband of 44 years on the grounds of irreconcilable personal differences, and was immediately granted her last wish . . .

Bus stop

Much-married Glynn Wolfe is a man with a philosophy all his own about love and marriage and, more specifically, divorce.

'Marriage,' he says whimsically, 'is like a bus. You miss one and down the road comes another.'

He made that statement after admitting that things 'just didn't work out' with wife No. 26, an attractive divorcee 40 years his junior (he was a sprightly 96 at the time).

When motel owner Glynn married Christine Camacho in 1984 he declared: 'This marriage will last because Christine is older. None of my other wives was more than 22 years old when I married them.'

126

Announcing his decision to quit the new matrimonial nest three months later, the tireless Mr Wolfe, who claims to have fathered 40 children from his 26 marriages, declared that he would immediately start the search for wife No. 27, adding: 'I don't see any future living my life alone. One of these days I'm going to find the right woman.'

Sparky

Such is the ingenuity of Mr Duman Atwal, one would not be at all surprised to learn the chap emits sparks in the dark.

Take the time his wife refused him a divorce. Was he non-plussed? Not a bit of it.

He simply got some other woman to divorce him instead.

He stood there in court, swore blind she was Mrs A. and the judge said: Right, done. Here's your divorce. Only in legal jargon of course.

But a few weeks before the divorce was due to become absolute the real Mrs Atwal got to hear about it. Pretty soon the police got to hear of it too.

And in no time at all Duman, 33, from Forest Gate, East London, was back in court explaining himself. He and his pretend missus, Jasbir Birdi, both got off with suspended sentences.

Not surprising in the circumstances, Mrs Atwal came to think less fondly of her husband.

His lawyer revealed: 'The ultimate irony is that since the fake divorce proceedings Mrs Atwal has divorced Mr Atwal.'

A Californian woman won a divorce from her schoolteacher husband after telling the court that she was forced by her husband to answer 'Yes, sir' or 'No, sir' to all of his questions. If she failed to give the proper response, she told the judge, he spanked her with a clothes brush and made her say 'Yes, sir' 500 times . . .

Sit-down protest

Kenneth and Kay Weaver of Harrisburg, Pennsylvania, were a model couple. A model for a cartoon strip, that is.

He was your archetypal 10-stone weakling, the sort that when he isn't being henpecked by a nagging wife, gets sand kicked in his face by the local Charles Atlas.

She was the original fat lady, the one that picture postcard artists delight in using when extolling the joys of English seaside resorts to the folks back home.

So it came as no surprise when police, alerted to the fact that the weedy Mr Weaver had suffered more than somewhat after being sat on by his 20-stone wife during an argument about his drinking, arrived on the scene to find him dead.

The robust Mrs Weaver fared rather better, however, when D.A. Richard Lewis ruled that her husband's death, which was caused by 'asphyxiation due to chest compression', was accidental and that there was no case to answer.

Two time loser

Betrayed wife Safia Sheikh tried to win back her husband by puncturing his contraceptives; the idea being if she got pregnant he would stay with her.

Besides, 37-year-old Safia from Southgate, London, also wanted to show her rival there was still sex in her marriage.

But two-timing husband Ijaz, 41, refused to give up his new love, and Safia didn't get pregnant either. In the end she had to settle for the divorce court.

A Milan court granted a husband visiting rights to his dog after his wife won custody of the pet in a divorce case.

Double trouble

Honestly, some men ought to be locked up to halt their faithless ways. Others require something altogether more drastic.

We refer to one Barry McAuliffe, whose courting was considerably restricted on account of his being behind bars.

But even within the grey stone walls romance flourished and in due course he and Patricia, the sweetheart who visited him regularly, were wed in prison.

A heart-warming tale, you might say. Not quite. For Barry and Patricia are now divorced, on the grounds that he had behaved unreasonably.

She caught him with another woman in the visiting room.

Two-way stretch

. . . And how's this for a neat piece of role reversal.

Prisoner Alan Price was on remand in Oxford jail when somebody got the word to him that Linda Cooper, his common law wife, was dallying with another.

The new man in her life, he learned, was a certain Graham Collier.

Price was in no position to do anything about it until by one of those outlandish coincidences Collier too ended up in the same prison.

And in the very same cell.

Still Price said not a word. But when he found that Linda, the mother of his child, had taken to seeing Collier on prison visits, Price boiled over.

He wasn't half as boiling though as the jug of hot water he poured over his cell mate.

It might have given him some satisfaction; it also earned him an extra year inside for grievous bodily harm.

Immaculate concept

He was just the man she was looking for, a rare find indeed: strong, masculine and still, at the mature age of 50, a virgin.

Or so Mustafa Baqerian claimed.

It took less than two months, however, for the blushing bride to discover that the man of her dreams had been more chased than chaste.

A Tehran court took only a few minutes to grant her a divorce after hearing that Mustafa had already been married four times and had fathered no fewer than 17 children.

Happy landings

The fastest-ever divorce happened at 120mph some 12,500ft over California when parachute freaks Gene and Lynda Ballard literally fell out of love.

After 12 years of marriage the couple legally parted in a free-fall drop, with Gene's lawyer passing Lynda the official papers.

Seven friends joined in to witness the deed. Then Gene, 35, and Lynda, 31, held hands and kissed goodbyeeee!

Spare Ribs

By now you will have gathered what you need most in the mating game is a fairly robust sense of humour. One can only hope Al Pacino, Robert Redford and Robert Kerry, the Governor of Nebraska, were thus gifted.

What these three gents have, or rather had, in common was Debra Winger, the fetching star of the movie "Terms of Endearment." All three. were variously reported to be the man in her life.

Delicious Debra thought otherwise. Off she went and got herself hitched to actor Timothy Hutton. But she did not forget the spurned ones.

On the very eve of her wedding Debra sent Al, Robert and Robert a telegram apiece – telling each of them she wanted him to be the first to know

But now for some more even-handed humour . . .

Spare Ribs

Love thy neighbour

The phone rang when she was in the middle of doing the Hoovering.

'Hello,' said the strange voice. 'I'm your husband's sex therapist.'

All of which came as a surprise to the loving young wife who had never had any complaints in that direction.

She was even more surprised when the stranger advised her to go out and make love to the first man she saw – to relieve her husband's hang-up.

Being a dutiful wife, she forgot all about the housework and slipped into her sexiest underwear.

The first man she saw when she opened the back door was her new next door neighbour innocently mowing the grass.

She took him by the hand and led him unprotesting to bed. It all went just as the doctor ordered.

An hour later when her husband came home to Teaneck, New Jersey, she proudly told him what she had done.

'But . . . but, I haven't got a sex therapist,' stammered the outraged husband.

And as he charged out of the house intent on murder the terrified neighbour managed to get to his car and escape.

Eventually the whole episode was traced down to phone hoaxer Kenneth Cohen, a TV executive. The next time he rang the wife kept him talking while police tracked the call.

He was arrested and charged with sexual harassment.

A police spokesman said: 'The most perplexed person in this saga is the neighbour. He couldn't believe his luck. He thought he'd moved into that sort of neighbourhood.'

'The husband's made it up with him now that we have caught the weirdo.'

'Enjoying the most wonderful of honeymoons. Thank you for making it possible.' – **Postcard to Rev Rodney Dowson of Selsey, Sussex, from a couple he had married.**

135

His and Hearse

You won't find the last resting place of Eric Camp who died, aged 82, after a fall at his Baldock, Herts, home.

In his place you will find a woman interred there, and the name on the headstone is of one Marion Gardner. For such was Eric's last wish.

Ever since he was little, Eric had the feeling he somehow did not belong in a man's world, that he would be happier as an Erica, or to be more precise, as a Marion.

But he tried his best to adjust, even to the extent of becoming a husband and fathering three children.

It was only after the war and some 40 years of manhood that he conceded he had to become a she. Nothing doing, said the National Health Service. You can't have a sex change off the Welfare State.

Eric did the next best thing. He changed his name and became a fully-fledged transvestite.

When he had his fatal fall he was wearing a dress and tights. And instead of a shroud, Eric/Marion went to meet his/her Maker clad in a frock.

Shortly after the publication of their best-selling book on love, marriage and divorce, husband and wife sociology professors Bill and Elaine Walster, of Madison, Wisconsin, announced that they were divorcing after 17 years of blissfully happy togetherness. Explained Bill: 'We discovered that many of the things in our book were true of ourselves. I wanted to work and she just wanted to go out all the time.'

Puppy love

Maybe he should have got himself a gerbil or a goldfish instead.

Trouble was, Graham Boothman had a great, floppy adorable labrador, answering to the name of Butch. Next to his wife it was what he loved most in all the world.

Actually there was a bit of a question mark over who truly was his heart's desire. Until the fateful night Mrs B. made the

classic mistake of trying to find out. 'It's either me or the dog,' she demanded.

Whereupon Graham went walkies to cool off, taking old Butch with him of course. Four days and 200 miles later, the wanderers returned to Beighton, Sheffield, where Mrs Pat Boothman had swallowed her pride, and the adage 'Love me, love my dog'.

She said generously: 'I just didn't know he felt so strongly about Butch.'

A St Albans clergyman's wife had her credit card application returned marked 'Insufficient information' after she wrote in the space opposite Husband's Employer: God.

Seven year hitch

Somewhere in Lincoln is a gambler who, we bet, is being as nice as you like to his wife. After all, he's got a stake in her future.

For the unknown punter has laid a thousand quid at six-to-four against that his marriage will last longer than seven years.

He stands to collect £1,500 if he wins. And the betting shop has also promised him a two-week continental holiday for him and his wife. They're all heart, these bookies.

Meanwhile he's keeping the bet secret from his wife – in case they have a bust-up over it.

Love in a cold climate

Other couples hold hands. Sue and Dave Trelfall held the ends of a 40 ft length of string. And instead of murmured endearments they had to be content bawling their love across the intervening space.

It was all in the cause of science. Dave's ex-wife, you see, had volunteered him for the Common Cold Research Centre where guinea pigs are infected with bacteria.

It was her idea of a practical joke but Dave, a sporting sort by all accounts, went along with it anyway.

And while he was at the centre he espied a lovely young volunteer, Sue. 'It was love at first sight,' he later recalled.

But the researchers' ruled that volunteers must not come into close contact with each other during tests – hence the piece of string.

Anyway, when it was all over, Sue, 36, and Dave, a 41-year-old coach driver, finally tied the knot. But they still needed the string.

For, romantic, adorable fools that they were, the couple chose to spend their ten-day honeymoon at the Salisbury Centre – in splendid isolation from each other.

Grace and favour

Funny how you see things in a different light when you're starry-eyed with love. Just look at the Episcopalian Bishop of Aberdeen and Orkney, The Right Reverend Frederick Darwent.

A man of the highest moral scruples, was the Right

138

Reverend. Indeed, once he stalwartly refused to officiate at a divorcee's wedding, on the grounds that such unfortunates had no right to marry in church.

Thus it was with some surprise that his flock learned the 56-year-old widower had opted for his own cathedral, St Andrew's in Aberdeen, as the venue of his marriage to Rona Fraser.

Mrs Fraser, you see, was a divorcee.

But as the good bish explained at the time: 'My views have not changed. It all depends on the situation you find yourself in.'

And that's the gospel truth.

Y not?

This story may well be apocryphal, but our informant swore to it: staff at Belfast's Corporation Street dole office became used to the weekly visits of an illiterate woman who signed for her social security payments with a laboured X.

Until the week she attempted instead a shaky Y. When a counter clerk appeared nonplussed, the woman explained: 'I've got married.'

Love me, love my frog

The Night of The Iguanas, Plymouth-style, wasn't at all the way Richard Burton and Ava Gardner made it out to be in the movie.

Mind you, Richard Burton didn't have anything against iguanas while Bob Newing couldn't stand the sight of them.

So when pet-loving wife Wendy chose to move ten of the things into their bedroom, Bob walked out.

'He didn't like the thought of all those eyes watching his every move,' she moaned.

You would have thought that after all these years he might have got used to them, might even have started liking the little fellows, and slipped them the occasional dead mouse or something.

139

But no. Bob was fed up to the back teeth with all manner of creepy crawlies. And Wendy appears to have cornered the market in them.

At the last count she had – wait for it – ten iguanas, four toads, two black widow spiders, a python, two water monitors, sundry lizards, God knows how many rats and mice and a plague of locusts.

Even Noah was content with two of each.

They didn't just arrive overnight, you understand. Vet's secretary Wendy had gradually built up her menagerie over 13 years of marriage.

And Bob had ample warning of her fondness for anything with scales on – on their honeymoon she brought along a grass snake and a tree frog for company.

Wendy said: 'Unfortunately he's not terribly fond of animals and it didn't help when my six-foot-long python bit him. Now, he's just had enough.'

Bob's walk-out meant Wendy had to get rid of her £1,000 collection. She said: 'I won't have room for them in future as we're selling the house. As well as the python I've got water monitors which grow up to nine feet long and need a room all of their own.

'I'm keeping my favourites like the tarantulas and red-eyed tree frog. I couldn't live without them.'

Bob, 50, certainly could. He said: 'You could say the animals were the Achilles' heel of our relationship.'

140

A Bloemfontein, South Africa, wife won a divorce from her boorish husband after he built a wall through the middle of their home and ordered her to stay on her side. And she wasn't even a different colour.

Silly Billy

When his marriage soured and all pleasure paled, a Kenyan sought help from his doctor. His witch doctor, that is.

And with that gentleman's unique skill the husband contrived to bewitch his ex-missus so she could no longer find comfort in the arms of another.

It worked, too – to such an extent that the green-eyed partner was instructed by a court to undo the spell.

Just for good measure he was also ordered to contribute a goat, whose sacrificial blood would be used to restore his ex-wife to her healthy heterosexual self.

A mere snip

What with all the fireworks and flags and frolics, the Americans probably never even noticed Tek Kor's extravagant gift to them.

He had a vasectomy.

Just in case anyone remains unimpressed, may we add that Kor, a top man in Thailand's meatball business, is also Bangkok's most-famed husband and father.

If you had seven wives and 22 children you would be pretty famed too.

Anyway, Kor, fed up making meatballs for that little lot, felt it was time to call a halt and he agreed to have a snip op.

A prudent man, he first sought counsel from an astronomer who advised him the most propitious date would be July 4 – America's Independence Day.

A beaming Kor announced to an unlistening world: 'It will be a present to the American people.'

Never mind, his seven wives were probably a lot more grateful.

141

GREAT HONEYMOON DISASTERS BY SIMON WELFARE

A hilarious collection of true stories about the extraordinary calamities that have befallen newly-married couples:

The bridegroom who was arrested for breaking into a contraceptive machine . . .

The dog who swallowed a golden wedding ring . . .

The bride who gave birth in a pew . . .

These are just some of the stories in this comic compendium. Even the great and famous have suffered on their wedding nights: Catherine the Great's husband preferred playing toy soldiers on the sheets rather than macho manoeuvres underneath them, while Napoleon was bitten on his Imperial left calf by Josephine's poodle as he was making love to his newly wed. GREAT HONEYMOON DISASTERS will bring comfort to those people who have always believed that surviving the honeymoon is the hardest part – after that, even married life is easy.

0 552 13199 7

BACHELORS' BUTTONS BY SONYA MILLS

Suddenly you find yourself on the doorstep. *She* has finally decided the time has come for you to look after yourself. Panic rises in your throat; you're going to be a flat dweller, you'll have to perform mind-boggling tasks like washing and ironing, cooking, setting the alarm clock *and* making sure you get out of bed in time for work.

But don't despair – BACHELORS' BUTTONS may just save your sanity – and your reputation.

Be honest – do you really know how to fry an egg without scrambling it, use a vacuum cleaner, manage a household budget, organise an edible dinner for two or make your one decent shirt look like it's been in the washing machine, not the food blender? No matter how modest or ambitious your home-making ideas, BACHELORS' BUTTONS is *the* survival guide for the domestically uninitiated.

Women need it too! Desert the ranks of the safety-pin brigade, learn that under the bed is not a bottom drawer and discover there's more to cooking than sticking a pie in the microwave.

BACHELORS' BUTTONS will preserve you from the disasters of independence and help make your home a happy refuge.

0 552 12723 X

A SELECTED LIST OF HUMOUR TITLES AVAILABLE FROM CORGI BOOKS

☐	13103 2	**A-Z of Street Cred**	*Christy Campbell*	£4.95
☐	11525 8	**Class**	*Jilly Cooper*	£2.95
☐	11751 X	**Jolly Super**	*Jilly Cooper*	£1.25
☐	11801 X	**Jolly Superlative**	*Jilly Cooper*	£1.25
☐	11752 8	**Jolly Super Too**	*Jilly Cooper*	£1.25
☐	11832 X	**Super Cooper**	*Jilly Cooper*	£1.25
☐	11802 8	**Super Jilly**	*Jilly Cooper*	£1.25
☐	12685 3	**Desert Island Biff**	*Chris Garratt & Mick Kidd*	£2.95
☐	99254 2	**Sincerely Yours (Biff II) (L.F.)**	*Chris Garratt & Mick Kidd*	£4.95
☐	99200 3	**Graffiti Omnibus Edition (H/B)**	*Roger Kilroy*	£7.95
☐	99137 6	**Graffiti 6**	*Roger Kilroy*	£1.50
☐	99045 0	**Graffiti 5: As the Actress Said to the Bishop**	*Roger Kilroy*	£1.75
☐	99022 1	**Graffiti 4**	*Roger Kilroy*	£1.50
☐	11812 5	**Graffiti 3**	*Roger Kilroy*	£1.50
☐	98116 8	**Graffiti 2**	*Roger Kilroy*	£1.50
☐	98079 X	**Graffiti: The Scrawl of the Wild**	*Roger Kilroy*	£1.75
☐	12723 X	**Bachelors' Buttons**	*Sonya Mills*	£3.95
☐	12796 5	**One Man and His Bog**	*Barry Pilton*	£1.95
☐	12791 4	**Any Fool Can Be A Villager**	*James Robertson*	£2.50
☐	12560 1	**Any Fool Can Be A Countryman**	*James Robertson*	£1.75
☐	12399 4	**Any Fool Can Be A Pig Farmer**	*James Robertson*	£1.75
☐	13199 7	**Great Honeymoon Disasters**	*Simon Welfare*	£1.95